In Defence of Astrology

Answer the Critics of Astrology

Robert Parry

quantum

LONDON • NEW YORK • TORONTO • SYDNEY

quantum

An imprint of W. Foulsham & Co. Ltd
The Publishing House, Bennetts Close, Cippenham, Slough,
Berkshire, SL1 5AP, England

ISBN 0-572-03059-2

Cover photograph by Jurgen Ziewe

A CIP record for this book is available from the British Library

Printed in Great Britain by Creative Print and Design (Wales), Ebbw Vale

In Defence of
Astrology

Answer the Critics of Astrology

To the ancestors for their wisdom and perseverance, and to Ruby

Robert Parry is a writer and practitioner of oriental medicine and a keen enthusiast of astrology and astronomy. Having also worked as a consultant astrologer, he remains a member of the Astrological Association of Great Britain and a Diploma holder with the Faculty of Astrological Studies.

Acknowledgement
The author and publisher wish to thank the Faculty of Astrological Studies for permission to reproduce its Code of Ethics on page 49.

Illustrations by the author

Contents

Introduction

This book is intended for anyone with an interest in what I believe to be one of the greatest, most enduring and most exciting ideas known to humankind. It is for anyone with just the tiniest glimmer of faith in a meaningful universe in which he or she has a part to play, no matter how small, no matter how humble. It is for anyone who does not believe that life is simply the outcome of blind and brutal forces of chaos and chance. It is for those who do not wish to use the materialistic straight-jacket that we are forced to wear each day as an excuse for dullness or stifling cynicism. It is for all those who believe in the dignity of the human spirit. It is for those interested in astrology.

In these pages I am not seeking to 'prove' astrology. I do not believe such a thing is possible – no more than it is possible to disprove it. What I *do* believe, however, is that astrology constitutes an international language, a symbolic collective consciousness that is not only inspirational in its message but also readily comprehensible to all. Astrology enables people the world over to realise how much they have in common, a shared experience that can transcend regional, religious and political boundaries in a way that is quite unique and which therefore needs to be preserved, perhaps more so than ever today in these troubled times.

We are, at heart, all of us, astrologers. Whether we realise it or not, or whether we *like* it or not, we all have the experience of the sky, the Earth beneath us and the cycles of the days, months and seasons deeply programmed into our psyches, part of our mental software since time began. It is this experience of the natural world, its rhythms and changes, which once shaped the most ancient cultures and philosophies, and which still shape the most modern patterns of human behaviour, feelings and desires today. The sky above is important and we neglect it at our peril. Shut off from the natural world, we can become sick, disoriented and lost. The rapport of humankind with the environment is essentially our experience of the skies, and this is the individual's claim to the title astrologer, as I shall be using the term in this book. For if, indeed, we are all travellers on the spaceship Earth, then we all need to be navigators of a sort, as well, and to avoid the hazards that others, whether by ignorance or by design, place in our path. Welcome. This book will help you defend yourself, and make your position clear.

If much of what follows here reads a little like a manual on practical self-defence techniques, it is no accident. In a respectful but light-hearted kind of way it is intended to do just that, because if we take a look at some of the great systems of self-defence that come from the East, such as the 'soft' martial arts of tai chi or akido, we discover that the masters achieve their legendary powers not necessarily through aggression, but through a combination of inner knowledge, relaxation and self-control. Through knowledge and relaxation comes anticipation; and through anticipation comes correct and perfect reaction. We can make use of these skills. They need not be reserved only for physical self-defence.

Enthusiasts of astrology often find themselves confronted by others who are hostile to their cause – and, oddly enough, by people displaying the same unfortunate degrees of irrationality and ignorance that they mistakenly level against astrologers themselves. The ability to defend oneself against this kind of ill-informed criticism comes not only through knowledge, but also through clarity, and perhaps a similar degree of self-confidence and relaxation as found in the ancient philosophies and martial arts of the East. The cultivation of such preparedness, along with the necessary arguments of defence that sustain it, is what you will find in these pages.

Real astrology, as distinct from show-biz and journalistic horoscopes which many people still wrongly associate with the subject, remains rather a remote activity in our times. And the feverish search for 'proof' and scientific respectability that is currently in vogue among professionals in the field is not really of much help to the public either, being comprehensible only to a handful of statisticians and specialists. Sometimes, too, astrologers will feel no need to defend themselves at all, or give reasons, if compelled, for an interest in such a strange and, to many, utterly *daft* occupation. The astrologer might feel able to bluff a way out or simply refuse, rather pompously, to discuss the matter at all.

'Give you a reason on compulsion! If reasons were as plentiful as blackberries, I would give no man a reason upon compulsion,'
Falstaff. Shakespeare's *Henry IV, part I*

Enthusiasts of astrology who fall into the same mould do neither themselves nor the subject much credit. And to an opponent who is a confirmed cynic, such a posture looks highly suspect. On the other hand, if you are a follower of astrology, or indeed a professional in the field, it is actually quite useful to be able to give reasons sometimes, to able to explain and argue for astrology on a conversational level, and in a way that is easily understood. This means debate, lively discussion and a little humour as well. And if it is apparent that the general public needs to learn more about 'real' astrology from time to time, then it seems equally apparent that astrologers must teach and communicate in a language both modern and comprehensible. Yes, this book is intended to inform and, if possible, to educate; but above all else it is here to be enjoyed. Inordinate seriousness and gravity are not the ways to overcome those critical to your cause. Nor should the discussion of great ideas, even those of the most profound kind as expressed within the compass of astrology, ever be incompatible with simple good cheer.

It is a pretty obvious fact of life that those who cannot laugh at themselves will usually encounter plenty of others willing to do the job for them. So please be inspired, please be informed by this humble offering. But above all, do smile, and do enjoy!

PART ONE

What is Astrology?

CHAPTER 1

The Experience of Astrology

Very slowly the sky darkens, leaving a purple glow along the silhouetted horizon. One by one, tiny jewels of light appear, the brightest and greatest first, until very soon the entire sky is filled with stars. Perhaps a bright planet or two will be shining out, or the great pearl of the Moon vying with the mysterious glow of our own galactic wheel, the Milky Way. Why do we so often pause and look up at the sky before hurrying indoors on such a night? Why at such times do lovers positively ooze tenderness, or children gaze from bedroom windows long past bed time? Why do old crooners urge us to fly them to the moon and 'sing among the stars' or an entire global souvenir industry suddenly spring up overnight at the return of a famous comet? Why do thousands of amateur-guided telescopes turn skywards each evening from every part of the globe, or inebriated travellers at sea, far from home, suddenly look up and wax poetical at the night sky? – as in this little piece by the writer Thomas Mann:

'"The stars! Oh, by the Lord, look at the stars!" a voice suddenly said, with a heavy sing-song accent. It belonged to a young man who had been Tonio Kröger's neighbour at dinner in the salon. His dress was very simple, his eyes were red, and he had the moist and chilly look of a person who had just bathed. With nervous and self-conscious movements he had taken unto himself an astonishing quantity of lobster omelette. Now he leaned on the rail beside Tonio Kröger and looked up at the skies, holding his chin between thumb and forefinger. Beyond a doubt he was in one of the rare and festal and edifying moods that cause the barriers between man and man to fall; when the heart opens even to the stranger, and the mouth utters that which otherwise it would blush to speak …

'"Look, my dear sir, just look at the stars! There they stand and glitter. My goodness, the whole sky is full of theb! And I ask you, when you stahd and look up at theb, and realise that bany of theb are a hundred tibes larger thad the earth, how does it bake you feel? Yes, we have invented the telegraph and the telephone and all the triumphs of our bodern times. But when we look up there we have to recogdize and understahd that we are worbs, biserable worbs and dothing else. Am I right, sir or ab I wrong? Yes, we are worbs," he answered himself, and nodded meekly and abjectly in the direction of the firmament.'

from *Tonio Kröger* by Thoman Mann

Often it takes exceptional circumstances to open our eyes afresh to the miracle of the skies. Reactions range from awe and tranquillity, to a sense of insignificance and inferiority, depending on one's mood at the time. Some of us adore the night sky, others fear and dread it. Some people feel the need to immerse themselves in its vastness, others are aware of an equally persuasive urge to rationalise its mystery through the language of science. Often the pull of the skies is an unconscious one. Some people sleep-walk over rooftops, following the Moon. Others find its presence almost magnetic, irresistibly engaging without quite knowing how or why, particularly at times of emotional intensity and excitement – as one of the great novelists of the last century, D.H. Lawrence, described it, using an almost abstract language to evoke the sensations:

'As the dance surged heavily on, Ursula was aware of some influence looking in upon her. Something was looking at her. Some powerful, glowing sight was looking right into her, not upon her, but right at her. Out of the great distance, and yet imminent, the powerful, overwhelming watch was kept upon her. And she danced on with Skrebensky, while the great white watching continued, balancing all in its revelation.

'"The Moon has risen," said Anton, as the music ceased, and they found themselves suddenly stranded, like bits of jetsam on a shore. She turned, and saw a great white Moon looking at her over the hill. And her breast opened to it, she was cleaved like a transparent jewel to its light. She stood filled with the full Moon, offering herself. Her two breasts opened to make way for it, her body opened wide like a quivering anemone, a soft, dilated invitation touched by the Moon. She wanted the Moon to fill in to her, she wanted more, more communion with the Moon, consummation. But Skrebensky put his arm round her and led her away. He put a big dark cloak round her, and sat holding her hand, whilst the Moonlight streamed above the glowing fires.'

from *The Rainbow* by D.H. Lawrence

The Moon, of course, is continually popular with poets – often to the point of infatuation. That most visible of concepts in astrological lore, the Moon has always been associated with reflection, with receiving and retaining images and feelings – and thus its age-old correspondence with the metal silver, used in mirrors and photographic film. The old Romantic poets especially would perceive a reflection of their own restless spirits in the changing, wayward phases of the Moon.

'Art thou pale for weariness
Of climbing heaven, and gazing on the earth,
Wandering companionless
Among the stars that have a different birth, –
And ever-changing, like a joyless eye
That finds no object worth its constancy?'

Percy Bysshe Shelley

The poets speak our minds, the way we all instinctively feel at moments but cannot always put into rational terms. Of course we can choose to run from the irrational, as many do when the flame of passion and intensity seems too threatening. But we lose a part of ourselves when we do so, and we become poorer as a consequence – shut in behind the walls of 'realism' and sobriety that we build primarily against pain, but consequently against joy and inspiration as well.

Our experience of the skies, the astrological experience in its most fundamental form, is our love affair with life, with all of its pleasure and pain included. For if we can love our friends, our family, those closest to us who are, after all, just so much flesh and bones according to purely biological analysis, then is it really so strange to love our planet and the family to which it likewise belongs? To our Earth and the family of the skies we owe our very existence. Should we be averse to loving such entities, no matter how remote? Certainly, our present age, in its urgency for a new and popular ecological consciousness, needs to rekindle that particular old flame because surely even the most cynical among us, if he loves nothing else, loves himself – yet this too is a love affair with the skies ...

'The body of a man is his house; the architect who builds it is the astral world. The carpenters are at one time Jupiter, at another Venus; at one time Taurus, at another Orion. Man is a Sun and a Moon and a heaven filled with stars; the world is a man, and the light of the Sun and the stars is his body.'

Paracelsus

The connection with the skies has always been felt. The arts, the poetry and the symbolic languages of humankind have grown out of such blissful infatuation. The Moon, the Sun, and the wandering planets have all figured as sources of fascination and veneration from the very first times when people began to notice relationships between certain celestial occurrences and the moods and changes within themselves and their community. Men and women and their gods grew alongside each other as a result. As humans came to know the skies, so too did they come to recognise the various parts within themselves, their own consciousness. The gods came to personify these parts, the Sun, the Moon, Jupiter, Saturn, Mercury, Mars and Venus – each one in its turn a father or mother, a scholar or a wise old man, a winged messenger, a warrior or a lover – each one a reflection of a desire, a wish, a thought. As naturally as a man loved his wife, his children, his parents, their individual characters and the community to which they belonged, so too did he love the Earth beneath his feet – and the Sun and the Moon, and the great family of the skies that seemed to fill his spirit with such variety and diversification.

This closeness, this intimacy between the skies and the natural forces of the psyche was not just a primitive fantasy; it continued throughout history. We find it still wherever we look. We find it in the great megalithic stone circles of Europe whose founders were totally love-struck with the Earth and the skies and their place within it. We find it, too, in periods of great artistic flowering – in the wonderful paintings and sculpture of the Renaissance where the skies and their inhabitants – the gods – appear in legion in the frescoes, ceilings, churches, state and private buildings of every kind, looking down from a starry vault, a blue and golden hemisphere high above the profane world. The human vision then was naturally skyward, the individual's spirit naturally elevated towards the stars, which is perhaps why so many of the words in our language come from them: 'martial' (Mars), 'jovial' (Jupiter), 'mercurial' (Mercury), 'venal' (Venus), 'saturnine' and 'Saturday' (Saturn), 'Monday' and 'lunatic' (Moon/*Luna*) to name but a few. Even our greatest religious festival in the West coincides with the 'rebirth' of the Sun each year, when the solar disk begins visibly to increase in height above the horizon – Christmas Eve.

The veneration still continues, make no mistake about that. Only today, apart from those quick, surreptitious glances at the horoscopes in newspapers, most of us have slightly more furtive means of exercising our affections. For some it is 'the great outdoors' – camping, rambling, fishing by night; for some it is the 'occult' – magical ceremony, bare botties dancing in the Moonlight. For others it is a search for an all-embracing oblivion in alcohol or drugs, or actual lunacy itself. Then, for some, it is building a small telescope and sitting with hot-water bottle and thermos flask through long nights of patient observation: the amateur astronomers, bless us all! And let's not forget the UFO enthusiasts and the enormous publishing industry that has grown up to satisfy their needs. Even though most sightings have perfectly banal explanations, almost everyone has a UFO story to relate, with some even claiming to have been whisked away and made love to by amorous extraterrestrials. Devotion indeed!

Then, more seriously, remember that national flags, under which so many people have fought and died, often contain a star or draw upon the solar circle or the lunar crescent for their basic design – or else upon that other and most potent of astrological symbols, the cross.

Nearer to home, those in the advertising industry have long known the subliminal appeal of astronomical symbolism. Next time you watch commercial TV, just try counting the number of stars, suns or moons, of one sort or another that appear in advertisements. People are attracted by the skies; they are comforted, or disturbed, or enchanted – but they rarely ignore a burst of starlight on their TV screens, or a swift blessing from heaven. The very celebrities that appear on our screens, those heroes and even god-like figures we worship so avidly are called 'stars'. When we buy our lottery ticket perhaps we think of that great golden finger coming down from the heavens – 'It Could Be You!' Astrology sells.

But the astrological experience is also a direct one. We all feel it. At times we feel it a lot. Luck is a reality. I once knew a man who went right through the card at a race meeting one afternoon, then came up with one or two winning greyhounds the very same evening, went to celebrate at his local club afterwards, promptly won the jackpot on a fruit machine, and finally, while picking up some late-night take-aways, found a banknote on the pavement outside the shop!

Yes, that is what is called a lucky day. But of course the boot can be on the other foot. We all know the feeling: times when nothing, but *nothing* works out! Misfortune and sheer bad luck seem to dog us incessantly, with no rational explanation whatsoever. Who can deny such periods? As the Bard says …

'When sorrows come, they come not single spies,
But in battalions.'

from Shakespeare's *Hamlet*

Certainly we feel we have worked out the laws of chance quite well, the way the dice must fall; but as any professional gambler or financial speculator will tell you – real life experience does not always seem to concur. The fact of the matter is that once you start to look a little closely at real life, and real astrology as it seeks to interpret it, the laws of chance go straight out of the window. In their place, many highly interesting questions start to arise, questions that really won't go away, unless you choose to ignore the evidence there before your eyes.

Why, for example, are astrologers able to interpret the character of an individual by analysing the positions of the planets at the moment of birth? Why are they able to forecast those periods of outstandingly good or absolutely abysmal 'luck'? How is it that certain astrological principles are vindicated even in experimentation and statistical research? Why, and how, are certain specialist astrologers able to locate lost articles, or missing animals, or answer questions on the viability of relationships, contracts, business ventures or real estate? How do others predict economic cycles, and movements in the stock and commodity markets of the world? How are they able to do this time and time again as a matter of routine, and – what's more – earn a respectable living doing so day after day? Why, in brief, does astrology work?

These are interesting questions, and in asking them you are already on an equally interesting journey of independence and self-discovery. You have started to comprehend your place in the scheme of things, willing to admit you can control your destiny by understanding and moving intelligently within the currents and tides of nature, not battling against them like some monstrous spoilt child who demands the whole universe to revolve around his own selfish, material existence. Ask those questions, and you have already begun to rediscover the experience, the incredible, fascinating and hugely rewarding experience of astrology.

CHAPTER 2

Tools of the Trade

In this chapter we are going to take a brief look at some of the practicalities, the 'nuts and bolts' of real astrology as it has been practised throughout the centuries and, indeed, as it is largely still practised today.

There are various branches of astrology in existence at the present time. Discounting, as we must do, the usually worthless star-sign horoscopes found in newspapers and magazines, the most widespread variety is called natal astrology. This deals with the character of individual people and often attempts, with varying degrees of accuracy, to predict the future trends in their lives. In addition to this, the branch of astrology that deals with nations and large groups of people is called mundane astrology (after the Latin *mundus,* the world), while that which deals with separate questions concerning personal affairs, journeys, lost articles, etc., and attempts to provide definite and clear-cut answers to these, is called horary astrology (Latin *hora,* 'hour'). There is also a branch called electional astrology dealing with the right-timing of future events, such as the starting of a business, the laying of a foundation stone, etc. And finally there is financial astrology, which deals, just as the name suggests, with trends in economic affairs, stock markets and commodity prices. The general public relying on the equity and currency markets of the world to sustain their pensions and investments funds would be surprised at the extent to which this form of astrology is employed by private investors and even within some of the largest financial institutions. It was J.P. Morgan the great industrialist and financier of the formative days of the American economy who was said to have remarked that, 'millionaires don't use astrologers – billionaires do!' Studied by the most humble to the most prestigious among us, astrology has been a part of the mental tool-box of independent and original thinkers and of men and women of action throughout the ages. So you are in good company. Here's how it works.

The basis of all astrological endeavour is the birth chart (also called natal chart). This is an accurate map of the sky for the exact date, time and place of birth. Now, this can be the birth of a person, or it could be the birth of a nation, or of a limited company, or even of an idea or a question. The central principle of astrology is that the start of anything, that very special moment when something new comes into existence, is absolutely paramount in significance.

The moment of birth is like a seed, containing everything that is to come and to grow from that seed. The astrologer's work, therefore, is not unlike that of a botanist or an expert in horticulture. Careful examination can tell him quite a lot. A botanist will tell you the species by examining the seed; an astrologer will tell you the personality by examining the birth chart. The botanist will explain the kind of conditions in which the seed will flourish; the astrologer will speculate on what kind of work and environment will best suit his or her client. The botanist will tell you how the seed will grow, and what the mature plant or tree will look like; the astrologer will tell you the way events are most likely to unfold into the future – forecasting.

A Day at the Office

So just how is an astrologer's chart put together? What sort of information does it contain? Figure 1 shows the construction of a typical birth chart, stage by stage. We begin by freezing the moment in time at which our birth takes place. This is the situation in Figure 1a, basically a picture of the sky as it was at the time in relation to the Earth beneath it. Appearing against the known background of fixed stars, you have the Sun, in this case just setting in the west; the Moon high up in the southern sky; and finally some of the planets, of which there are nine in all including the Earth. The planets are our nearest neighbours in space, members of our solar system that shine by the reflected light of the Sun. The word *planet* actually means 'wanderer'. Many of them are easily visible to the naked eye if you know where and when to look. They will appear to change position from night to night while the stars, which are distant suns, stay the same and will retain the same formations in relation to one another. The planets are what astrologers take note of the most, much more than the fixed stars or constellations.

In Figure 1b you have the narrow band of stars called the zodiac marked in, divided up into its well-known and celebrated 'signs', twelve equal sections, within which all those important bodies, Sun, Moon and planets, are invariably situated. Of course, some of the signs and planets would have been out of sight and beneath the horizon at the moment of birth being described here, but these bodies are still considered, and they have now been included in our picture to complete the circle of

Figure 1a. Freezing a moment in time

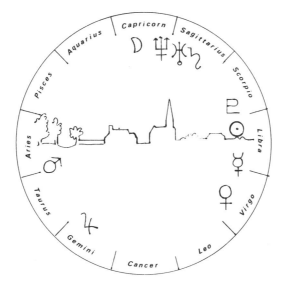

Figure 1b. The 'frozen moment' with the signs of the zodiac and the planets shown

the heavens. The planets themselves are now also shown in their traditional glyph form, the symbols recognised by astrologers the world over: Mercury (☿); Venus (♀); Mars (♂); Jupiter (♃); Saturn (♄); Uranus (♅); Neptune (♆); and Pluto (♇). Therefore, we have Mercury, Venus, Mars and Jupiter beneath the horizon in our illustration, and the other bodies, including the Sun and Moon, above it.

In Figure 1c the all-important horizontal axis of the chart has been added.

Roughly corresponding to the actual horizon in Figure 1a, this line joins the points where the zodiac meets the horizon in the East (called the Ascendant) and in the West (Descendant). Meanwhile, the local meridian – that great imaginary circle that passes overhead and joins the north and south points of the horizon – has also now been drawn in, creating the equally important vertical axis of the chart. This is marked MC/IC on the

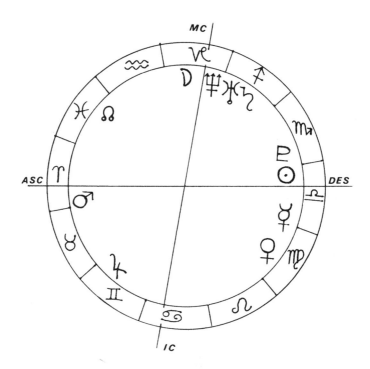

Figure 1c. The horizontal and vertical axes of the chart have been drawn in

chart, after their Latin terms *Medium Coeli* and *Immum Coeli*, respectively. Any planets found close to these lines are considered especially strong – like the Moon in this case, and the Sun also, which is almost on the horizon close to the Descendant.

By the time we get to Figure 1d we have something approaching the finished chart, as most astrologers would recognise it. Some added features have appeared here, namely the houses of the chart. The houses are sections of space, again twelve in number, which begin at the chart's rising degree, or Ascendant, and which extend right around the 'clock' to cover the entire sky. There are many systems for dividing the chart in this way, but the one shown here is one of the most commonly used, the Placidus House System, named after its seventeenth-century inventor. Houses, like the signs of the zodiac, are important, and the astrologer will look closely at the placement of each planet by both house and sign when judging the quality and character of the whole chart.

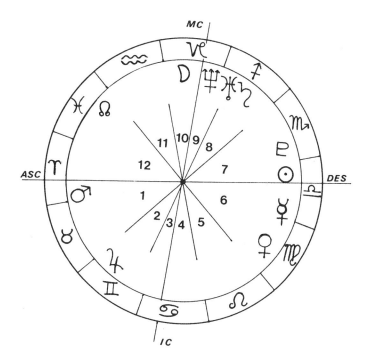

Figure 1d. The final chart includes the twelve astrological houses

Figures 2 and 3 (see pages 28 and 29) show two typical working charts, as you would find them on the astrologer's desk. You know what to look out for by now. Firstly there are the planets (for convenience, the Sun and Moon are called planets in astrology) with their exact positions marked in degrees and minutes. These co-ordinates can be listed separately, as in Figure 2, or they can appear inside the chart wheel itself, as in Figure 3. Always there is the circle of the zodiac, the twelve star-signs from Aries through to Pisces, shown on the outer rim; and finally there is the system of houses, the divisions within the wheel – like spokes radiating from the centre.

The sky is always changing, of course, as the Earth rotates beneath it, turning once on its axis every twenty-four hours, so that all these positions can vary, not only from hour to hour but from minute to minute, giving rise to any number of possible birth charts. For example, if you refer back to Figure 1 for a moment, and imagine the chart, say, ten minutes onwards in time, Mars would then be rising, placed no longer in the 1st house but in the 12th, while the Sun would have set beneath the horizon, no longer in the 7th house but now in the 6th. These changes can make a big difference, which is why we each have a distinct and unique astrological make-up, each born at our own particular place and time.

The planets themselves are also in constant motion against the background of the zodiac. Their individual speeds vary greatly. The ever-changing Moon, for example, makes one complete circuit of the zodiac in around twenty-eight days, while the 'wise old man' of the zodiac, Saturn, takes as long as thirty years. Each planet, moreover, has a distinct and definite character, which is modified by the sign and house in which it is placed. Mars, for example, is the planet of sexuality, extraversion, aggression and self-confidence. It has numerous associations – for example with the sign Aries, the metal iron, with fire, the colour red and with the ruby. So, in this instance, Mars's nature would be considered stronger or more forthright when found in Aries rather than, say, in the opposite sign of the zodiac, Libra. The same goes for all the other planets and their signs. The table on page 27 lists just a few of these features, 'correlations' as they are called.

Planet	Qualities	Colours	Metal	Stones
Moon	Imagination, Fantasy, Reflection, Thought	White, Sea tones	Silver	Moonstone, Pearl
Mercury	Communication, Business Agility, Craft	Variegated, yellow	Quicksilver	Onyx, Beryl
Venus	Comfort, Love, Desire, Beauty, Proportion	Blue, Green	Copper	Sapphire, Aquamarine
Sun	Splendour, Creativity, Pride, Diplomacy	Yellow, Red	Gold	Topaz, Garnet
Mars	Force, Aggression, Courage, Sexuality	Red	Iron	Ruby, Diamond
Jupiter	Joy, Expansion, Law, Preservation, Philosophy	Green, Purple	Tin	Emerald, Marble
Saturn	Age, Tradition, Slowness, Death, Limits	Black	Lead	Lapis, Quartz
Uranus	Change, Revolution, Originality, Invention	Metallic colours		
Neptune	Mystery, the Unconscious, Illusion, Inspiration	Camouflage		
Pluto	Power, Hidden Forces, Implacability, Destiny	Hidden		

Angular relationships between planets are also very important. These relationships are called 'aspects' in astrological jargon. An aspect blends the characteristics of bodies in certain special ways. For example, a square (90-degree) aspect between two planets indicates tension or disagreement between their natures, whereas a trine (120-degree) aspect indicates sympathy and co-operation (see Figure 4). There are about a dozen different types of aspect, each corresponding to a precise division of the circle. Figure 3 has the aspects for that particular chart listed in the square grid to the lower right of the chart wheel.

As we have seen, the zodiac itself contains twelve signs: Aries, Taurus, and so on. An important point is that these signs are distinct from the old star groups that are still referred to in astronomical maps and textbooks. These star groups, or constellations as they are called, can bear the same names as the popular signs of the zodiac but they are based on different co-ordinates. This is because the astrologer's zodiac actually moves with time, albeit very gradually from year to year, as seen against

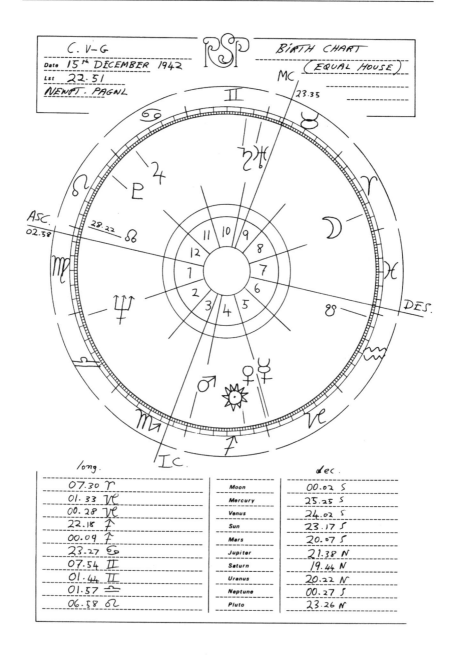

Figure 2. Typical example of a birth chart as an astrologer would draw it. The co-ordinates of the planets and signs of the zodiac are listed in the table

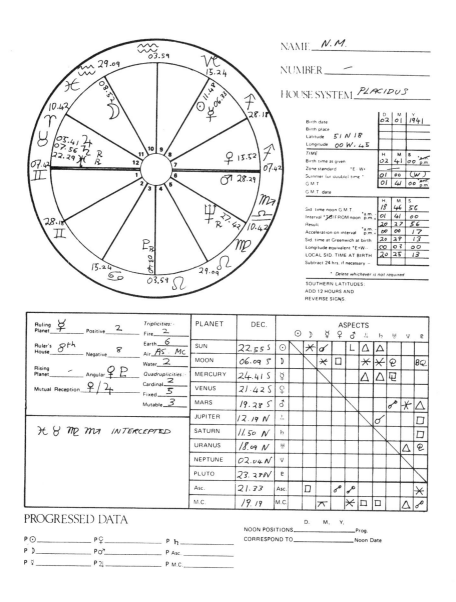

Figure 3. A further example of a typical birth chart. The co-ordinates of the planets and the signs of the zodiac are shown inside the chart wheel itself

29

the background of fixed stars – ensuring, no matter what progressive variations occur between the relation of the Earth to the Sun, that the zodiac always stays in touch with the passage of the seasons: spring, summer, autumn and winter.

Collectively, the twelve zodiac signs themselves have many sub-divisions. First there is that seasonal division into what are called Cardinal, Fixed and Mutable signs; then there are six positive and six negative signs; and also there is the division of the signs into elements: Fire, Earth, Air and Water. All these features help to determine the unique character of any planet located within the boundaries of that sign, and make for innumerable possible permutations.

Suffice it to say there is an awful lot that the astrologer has to keep in mind, and long ago it was found that the easiest way to remember all the possible permutations was to employ a simple mnemonic device for each sign, usually an animal or creature of some kind.

And what about the houses? Well, each of these actually corresponds to a particular field of human activity. For example, an astrologer looks to the house placement of each planet to locate the area of life in which it will most likely manifest, whether in career (10th house), or in partnerships (7th house),

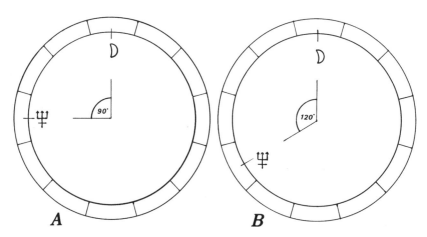

Figure 4. a) Example of a 90-degree angle of separation between two planets, or square aspect. b) Example of a 120-degree angle of separation between two planets, or trine aspect

or with family (4th house), and so on. Every human activity, every facet of being alive has its place under one of the twelve houses. The origins of these correspondences are historical in nature, but like the zodiac they are actually based on geographical co-ordinates and the time-honoured associations with the four quarters of heaven and, therefore, also the four seasons. Because of this, and despite many assertions to the contrary, they do follow a strictly logical pattern. The table below shows some of the main correlations for each house. For instance, the rising degree at the time of birth, or Ascendant is always considered to be a very personal point in the chart for any individual – and so this marks the beginning of the 1st house. Meanwhile, its opposite point, the descending degree and cusp of the 7th house, will describe the 'opposite number' in life – the partner, or enemy. Similarly, the highest point in the chart, the MC, which is always indicated by the position of the Sun at noon for the locality in question, is naturally associated with the idea of 'going forth' and therefore of the individual's place and standing in the world – in other words their career. This is the point that marks the cusp of the 10th house – while the opposite place in the chart, the IC, which is the location of the Sun at midnight beneath the horizon, indicates the cusp of the 4th house – the home and place of retreat and rest.

Section	Seasonal quality	Element	Polarity	Mnemonic device
1	Cardinal	Fire	Positive	A ram (Aries)
2	Fixed	Earth	Negative	A bull (Taurus)
3	Mutable	Air	Positive	Twins (Gemini)
4	Cardinal	Water	Negative	A crab (Cancer)
5	Fixed	Fire	Positive	A lion (Leo)
6	Mutable	Earth	Negative	A young woman (Virgo)
7	Cardinal	Air	Positive	Scales (Libra)
8	Fixed	Water	Negative	A scorpion (Scorpio)
9	Mutable	Fire	Positive	An archer (Sagittarius)
10	Cardinal	Earth	Negative	A goat (Capricorn)
11	Fixed	Air	Positive	Water pourer (Aquarius)
12	Mutable	Water	Negative	Fishes (Pisces)

House	Location in the chart (northern hemisphere)	Field of activity
1st	East, Place of Sunrise	Self, Appearance, Image, Beginnings
2nd		Material affairs, Finance, Resources
3rd		Communications, Early learning, Brethren, Study
4th	North, Midnight	Inner experience, Home, Parents
5th		Creativity, Children, Speculation, Recreation
6th		Service, Care, Health
7th	West, Place of Sunset, Opposite the 1st	Partners, Rivals, Opposites, the 'Other Self'
8th	Opposite the 2nd	Resources of others, Death, Inheritance
9th	Opposite the 3rd	Expansion, Travel, Wisdom
10th	South, Sun at noon, Opposite the 4th	External Sphere, Reputation, Career
11th	Opposite the 5th	Ambitions, Friendships, Shared Principles
12th	Opposite the 6th	Privacy, Secrets, Restrictions, Guilt

The distinct and diverse astrological nature of every human being on this Earth is a result of all these factors combining: planets, houses and signs. A useful metaphor is to think of a stage production. The planets are the actors; the houses make up the scenery; and the zodiac is the theatre in which it all takes place. As stated already, the permutations, the possibilities are endless.

Later on, we are going to look at the way astrologers make use of this kind of information, firstly to judge character and personality from the chart, and secondly to speculate on future trends by expanding and developing the chart in certain ways. But as you can see already, it is absolutely essential, imperative, for the astrologer to have access to precise birth data, including the exact time and place as well as the date. This is why horoscopes in magazines and papers are of little value, using only the Sun signs of its readers, in other words the month of birth only (regardless of even the year!) as a basis for so-called predictions. The one good thing about Sun-sign journalism is that it does at least get people to think and to realise that the future is something that could be open to change. It can also provide entertainment and a certain positive familiarity with the inner world of symbolism and the imagination, a kind of 'people's psychology'. Arguably this is better than nothing. But as a predictive tool, and as a means of self-understanding it is of little value because individual charting is completely impossible under such circumstances.

So there you have it. Genuine astrology is not to be found in the Sunday supplements or, sadly, even on television or radio. The real thing – and you've already taken a glimpse of it here – is a professional enterprise with a long and distinguished history, and an even more exciting present. This is what we are going to look at next: all part of our determined bid to answer that most intriguing of questions, 'What is Astrology?'

CHAPTER 3

From Magic to Mockery

Picture the scene. It is Sunrise on a chilly day in late winter. It seems as if the entire community, anyone who is anybody, is gathered here on the vast plains about the circle of stones. The elders and wise women have been vigilant, as they always are, and always have been. This morning they will know exactly where the Sun will rise, exactly how the great Moon will appear. The calendar and oracle speak through the stones to them; the heavens dictate the time for planting the seed, and the new year's crops will be sown. The ceremony proceeds: the sacrifice, the music, the chanting. The Earth beneath seems to resonate with the importance and the magic of the moment. Later there will be dancing and festivities, and priests will attend to the observatory, adjusting wooden marker stakes, taking measurements, discussing the latest developments and progressive changes that they and their ancestors have noted in the skies over millennia of seasons coming and going.

Thousands of years ago, before we have any real records of history to go by, this might well have been the picture in so many parts of Europe on such important occasions throughout the year. Other places on the globe would have enjoyed their own particular local observances: whole communities clustered around temples, pyramids, sacred groves, churches; always oriented to the cardinal points, always aligned with the Sun and the great turning wheel of the sky above. The world was one of magic, veneration, love for nature and a determination to understand and work within its inscrutable framework of time and change. Here is the origin of the astrological experience: surely as much in friendship and love as in fear and superstition.

I, for one, have always felt dissatisfied with the usual explanation provided by historians for pursuits such as magic, religion or astrology. We are urged to believe that the main driving force behind ancient prehistoric communities and their sky-oriented cultures was fear. Fear ruled everything. The gods of nature were worshipped and propitiated through fear. Temples and great stone circles were erected through fear. Fear gave rise to every personification of every natural force, from thunder and lightning to the seasons themselves. What nonsense! Although insecurity was certainly felt at times of war or natural disaster, the fear-principle is grossly overstated in our conventional view of antiquity. Perhaps this is owing to our present attitude to life, and the dreadful and unprecedented uncertainties that characterise our own culture and times. It is an attitude and an approach to history that is forgivable, but it tells us little of those who have gone before.

Conventional scholarship leans towards the view that astrology began in the old Mesopotamian civilisations of the Middle East sometime around the second millennium BC. But this is by no means universally accepted among all historians, nor among astrologers themselves. All we really know is that astrology emerged visibly around this time as a system that had already reached a high standard of complexity, hinting, therefore, at a much older origin. In fact, it may already have peaked and fallen into a degenerate and decadent phase by the time it seeped into popular usage in the superstitious worlds of the late Egyptian and Babylonian civilisations.

Our involvement with the skies is perhaps as old as the human species itself. There is evidence of the phases of the Moon being recorded via notches on bone as early as 15,000 BC. Much later, there is evidence of a preoccupation with astrology in the ancient Vedic and Taoist literature of India and China, and, as we have seen, in the megalithic stones of north-west Europe, which have now been shown beyond any shadow of doubt to have been highly sophisticated observatories as well as religious sites. All these have as great, if not a greater claim to antiquity than Babylonian astrology. The stone circles of Avebury and Stonehenge in England, for example, are currently thought to date from around 4,000–2,000 BC.

However, it is from the Mesopotamian and the later classical cultures of Greece and Rome that most of our modern astrological system is derived. The spread of astrology to the Greek and Roman worlds occurred in the centuries immediately prior to the Christian era, and here it was that the birth chart as we know it, began to take shape, so that by the time of Manilius and Ptolemy, that is by the first and second centuries AD, the astrologer's work is quite recognisable and familiar to those in practice today.

In those times, astrology went hand in hand with many other disciplines which we would nowadays consider unconnected. Medicine, for example, was deeply entwined with astrological lore. The great second-century physician Galen, for example, used his doctrine of the four humours extensively. These were also the four elements of astrology, and influenced medical thought for centuries. Chinese medicine is still based on an observation of the elements and how these apply to the various organs and functions within the human body.

Astronomy was also part of the astrological tradition at that time, being simply the mathematical branch of the subject. There was no bitter distinction between the two as there is today. Astrology and astronomy were taught side by side at academic centres throughout the civilised world, united with subjects as diverse as philosophy, music, architecture, politics, agriculture and the arts. With the decline of Rome and the gradual emergence of the dark ages in Europe, it was the Islamic world that continued the astrological tradition. Many of the star names we use today come from it, and the Islamic culture further refined the whole process of observation, compiling more and more accurate tables of projected planetary movements, called ephemeredes. Astrology, meanwhile, continued to flourish in India and China, with a growing cross-fertilisation of ideas between East and West taking place in those lands.

With the European Renaissance came perhaps the greatest flowering of astrological inventiveness. Here many branches of the art reached their peak of excellence and popularity. There was still little antagonism between astrology and the Church at this time, moreover, and many leading figures in the ruling establishment, including the Pope, understood and welcomed the use of astrology in their own affairs as much as in the secular world. Astrological medicine was taught at centres such as Padua in Italy, while in Florence and Rome the blending of classical and humanist ideals, all permeated with astrological lore and symbolism, inspired some of the greatest achievements in the arts and sciences.

Many famous and celebrated figures of the times employed their own astrologers, the fabulous courts of the Medici family, for example. We also know that Elizabeth I of England commissioned the astrologer and scientist Dr John Dee to determine the most propitious date for her coronation. Astrology was used extensively for revealing character, answering questions, locating missing persons or goods, speculating on the course of military campaigns and for judging relationships of all kinds. During the English Civil War, astrologers worked with the armed forces of both sides. One of these was William Lilly who later found himself in considerable trouble with the authorities for predicting the great fire of London in 1666 with such accuracy that some thought he might have had a hand in starting it! Astrology was at its zenith in these times. It touched the lives of all, from the highest of courtiers to the humblest of citizens.

By the late sixteenth century, however, astrology in the West was already in decline. The spirit of the Enlightenment had produced a new found confidence in man's powers over nature that temporarily eclipsed the by-then slightly decadent pronouncements of astrologers. The penny almanacs, the forerunners of today's Sun-sign journalism, were widely distributed at that time on almost every street corner; many of these were of highly questionable quality and authenticity, and did little to endear astrology to the newly emerging intelligentsia. Astrology, and particularly astrology as a means of forecasting events, lost much of its intellectual credibility, appearing to be unscientific and outside the normal techniques of experimentation and replication – which, indeed, to many of its critics it is still to this day.

The rise of maritime power and commerce, which used the stars for chronology and navigation, and hence for making money, was perhaps an additional factor in the decline, as was the seventeenth century's penchant for burning at the stake all witches, and indeed anyone remotely connected with the occult. Astrology went underground for a while, at least until the early nineteenth century. When it did re-emerge it was all the stronger for the experience of self-examination and stringent reappraisal that had by necessity taken place.

In our own times, there has been a vast resurgence of interest in the subject and it is today as popular and widespread as ever, not only through the rather questionable practice of pop astrology, but also among intellectuals and professional people the world over who understand and use serious, chart-based astrology sensibly and prudently to help plan and manage their daily affairs. Today, also, much of the emphasis has shifted to a scientific approach and recent research has provided persuasive evidence for at least some of astrology's long-cherished traditions. Before looking at modern trends in astrology, however, it might be of interest to consider once again for a moment the long and impressive pedigree that sustains it. For indeed some of the most brilliant and influential men and women on the stage of world history have studied, supported and encouraged the subject. Here is a by no means exhaustive list of distinguished persons known to have been wholly or partly sympathetic to astrology:

Abelard, Peter; Aeschylus; Albertus Magnus; Alcuin; Alexander the Great; Anaximander; Aquinas, St Thomas; Aristotle; Ashmole, Elias; Augustine, St (later anti); Averroes; Bacon, Francis; Bacon, Roger; Bede, the Venerable; Bernhardt, Sarah; Blake, William; Boehme, Jocob; Botticelli; Boyle, Robert; Brahe, Tycho; Bruno, Giordano; Byron; Caesar, Julius; Cromwell, Oliver; Charlemagne; Charles I of England; Charles II of England; Chaucer; Copernicus; Dante; Dee, John; Dryden, John; Duns Scotus; Durer, Albrecht; Elizabeth I of England; Emperor Augustus; Emperor Claudius; Emperor Domitian; Emperor Hadrian; Emperor Nero; Emperor Tiberius; Emperor Titus; Emperor Vespasian; d'Este, Isabella; Eudoxus; Franklin, Benjamin; Galen; Galileo; Genghis Khan; Goethe; Grosseteste, Robert; Henry VIII of England; Heraclitus; Herodotus; Hesiod; Hipparchus; Hippocrates (later anti); Hitler, Adolph; Holst, Gustav; Homer; Horace; Huygens, Christian; Jefferson, Thomas; Jung, C.G.; Juvenal; Kepler, Johannes; Luther (later anti); Macrobius; Marlowe, Christopher; Mary I of England; de' Medici, Catherine; de' Medici, Cosimo; de' Medici, Lorenzo; Miller, Henry; Milton; Morgan, J. P; Mussolini; Napoleon; Newton, Isaac; Nicolaus of Cusa; Nostradamus; Origen; Philip II of Spain; Plato; Pliny; Plotinus; Pope Alexander IV; Pope Calixtus III; Pope Clement VII; Pope John XX; Pope John XXI; Pope Julius II; Pope Leo X; Pope Paul III; Pope Sixtus IV; Posidonius; Proclus; Pythagoras; Regan, Ronald; Roosevelt, Theodore; Scott, Michael; Scott, Sir Walter; Schiller; Seneca; Shakespeare, William; Spinoza; Steiner, Rudolf; Tacitus; Thales; Twain, Mark; Virgil; Vitruvius; Wallenstein.

Modern Astrology: The Split Personality

Astrology has always existed at different levels of sophistication. There have always been good and bad astrologers. But today we have an almost schizophrenic state of affairs, with, on the one hand, the advent within the serious astrological community of numerous societies, teaching bodies and research teams of impeccable credentials, while, on the other hand, cheap, puerile star-sign columns appearing *ad nauseam* in every popular newspaper and magazine, and now of course on radio, TV and the internet. Never before has the standard been so high, or so low. Astrology now has its clowns and comedians as well as some of its most brilliant researchers and scientists; and not without justification do many now view its treatment within the popular media as little short of mockery.

This rebirth of astrology, with both its advances and its degeneration, begins around the turn of the last century with a newly growing interest in the subject in North America and Europe, especially in England and Germany. Within this revival certain important figures stand out. For instance, the great Swiss psychologist Carl Jung (1875–1961) was one of the first to recognise the importance of astrological symbolism in the study of the human mind. His concept of archetypes, autonomous forces ever-present in the human unconscious and often appearing as major themes in dreams, the arts, mythology and religion, found a natural historical parallel in planetary symbolism. Jung found that certain figures and mythical beings seemed to occur again and again in the dreams and emotional lives of his patients; the hero type, for example, or the wise old man, the trickster figure, or the Earth mother; or universal themes such as wisdom, sacrifice, virgin birth, mystical union of male and female, a flame or a sword beneath water, and so on.

All these themes could be found in the mythologies of ancient peoples, and in the classical arts. Yet men and women, often totally without academic knowledge or even basic education, would constantly reiterate these ideas in their dreams or under hypnosis. Moreover, these archetypes of the unconscious, as Jung called them, often became driving forces in the lives of perfectly sane and balanced individuals as well as those who were mentally disturbed. People were found to be inspired by them, to be influenced by them, and to fear them as well. The archetypes seemed to be something eternal, outliving individual men and women, and it was this that led Jung to the concept of the collective unconscious, something in which all peoples of all ages share, simply by virtue of being alive.

Jung found that the archetypes themselves could best be represented by ancient symbolism. Although superficially it appeared that different cultures at different historical periods enjoyed their own distinctive symbols and metaphors, closer examination proved that certain major themes were repeated throughout, ever-present in the human psyche. The great gods of the ancient and classical worlds, from Mesopotamia through to Greece and Rome, provided the richest sources of symbolism for Jung. The gods shared the same names with the planets: Jupiter, Saturn, Mercury, and so on. And this inspired Jung to study the subject of astrology more seriously. He often approached his patients through astrological symbolism, and also pioneered some experimental research into the astrology of relationships, studying many charts of married couples in search of planetary contacts between the two – 'synastry' as it is called.

Jung, even in his own time, was recognised as one of the foremost scholars of his century, and his stature has tended to grow rather than diminish with time. It was his example that, perhaps more than any other, helped to restore some of the respect that astrology had lost during the eighteenth and early nineteenth centuries.

Since Jung we have seen many landmarks in the progress of astrology: the founding of the Astrological Lodge of London (1917); the American Federation of Astrologers (1938); the Faculty of Astrological Studies (1948); the Astrological Association of Great Britain (1958) and the Association of Professional Astrologers International (1990), all highly successful bodies that have co-ordinated and raised the standards of professional practice, teaching and research throughout the world. In very recent times (2002) we also have the emergence of an MA degree in Cultural and Social Astronomy and Astrology at Bath Spa University under the auspices of the Sophia Project. The goal of the Sophia Project is to advance the scholarly study of astrology and cultural astronomy in British institutions of higher education – which, to date, also include universities at

Southampton, Canterbury and Leicester. Funds for this purpose are administered by the Sophia Trust, which is advised by a steering committee comprising trustees and elected representatives from the astrological community.

One of the projects fostered by the Sophia Project is the Research Group for the Critical Study of Astrology, whose role is to monitor standards of research and promote the use of sound scientific methods in empirical studies. These include studies not only by astrologers themselves, but also by their detractors, so that a fair and unbiased approach is assured.

Attempts to place astrology on a scientific footing through the use of genuine statistical or experimental evidence has a fairly brief history but one which has accelerated rapidly and impressively during the past forty years or so, culminating in our own times in the thorough, often quite remarkable and brilliant work of men such as the late Michel Gauquelin and John Addey who, in search of demonstrable proof of astrological principles, examined literally hundreds of thousands of individual charts and subjected these to rigorous analysis. The results of Gauquelin's work during the middle part of the last century, and which have since been replicated, have so far proved the most encouraging, already supplying demonstrable proof of at least some of the traditional tenets of astrological lore, namely his 'Mars effect', where this particular body, the planet of strength and aggression, features more often than chance would normally allow in the charts of eminent sportsmen and women. We will have more to say about Gauquelin's work later in this book (see Chapters 8 and 11) and of its possible value, or otherwise, for astrology today.

Meanwhile, following on from Jung's example, the birth chart has now become a recognised tool for many working within the counselling professions. As we have seen, the birth chart of the individual offers a remarkably accurate insight into the often largely hidden and unconscious traits of character and personality hidden within us all. Because of this, many modern astrologers are now qualified psychologists, and many psychologists are astrologers. The simple fact that counsellor and patient can sit down together and examine something as objective and as innocuous as an astrological chart on the desk in front of them, has proved to be an excellent point of departure, moreover, not only for the discussion of emotional problems experienced by the patient, but also for revealing any trauma and even illness that might have taken place in the past.

But, of course, alongside all these wonderfully exciting developments, there has also been in our times an abuse of astrology perhaps unparalleled in any other period of history. The first regular 'astrological' contribution to appear in the modern press dates from 1930 when an astrological profile on the latest royal baby was run in a popular English newspaper, *The London Daily Express*. This article was so well received that its author, R.H. Naylor, was invited to write a regular column. This was quickly emulated by other papers, all of which quickly realised that lengthy astrological analysis of individuals was far less likely to sell than brief superficial horoscope columns for all. The whole thing went downhill pretty fast and soon became the kind of tittle-tattle we are all familiar with today.

More recently, with the advent of breakfast programmes and other popular shows on TV and radio, there has come the new phenomenon of the show business astrologer. Such individuals can become household names, followed by millions with a strange mixture of attentiveness, amusement and contempt as they race breathlessly through all twelve star signs in rapid succession during their brief three-minute slot of air time. Yet – paradoxically – these people can also be practising consultant astrologers in their own right: working on finished charts for private clients, perhaps all the more successful for such exposure. Maybe, indeed, there is no such thing as bad publicity. Although such glitzy individuals are frequently a source of much grumbling and, to be truthful, not a little jealousy among the serious astrological community, the show business astrologer, along with his or her less glamorous cousins in the popular press, appears to be here to stay. From magic to mockery seems a long journey for astrology to have made over the millennia. Yet there is enchantment in laughter, and the ability to entertain others is perhaps not such a bad thing when all is said and done. It is also one which astrologers should perhaps not expel entirely from their ranks if they wish to retain some of the magic.

So by now it should be becoming evident that the answer to our question, 'What is Astrology?' has to be a two-fold or even a three-fold one. There is the scientific approach, the psychological approach, and the pop version. In order to continue our search it is now time, therefore, to look at the kinds of astrologers you are likely to encounter in the modern world, and the kinds of astrology they represent.

CHAPTER 4

Going to an Astrologer

The astrologer is a rare breed, sometimes difficult to locate, and equally as difficult at times to comprehend, risking slander, ridicule and misrepresentation to a quite staggering degree to ensure the continuation of the species. Contrary to what many seem to believe, however, astrologers are not particularly eccentric or odd. It is a profession, like any other. There are various standards within that profession, and some are higher than others; but by and large its members are intelligent, caring and trustworthy individuals going about their daily business while at the same time helping one or two people as they go.

The Good, the Bad, and the Ugly

When considering the many different kinds of astrologers at large in the world today, it might be helpful to divide their number into the following broadly-based categories:

a) Pop astrologers

b) Low-income professionals or small business persons

c) Private, semi-professional astrologers

d) Fully professional consultants.

Most people have contact with astrology through newspapers, magazines, TV or radio. This is the work of the so-called pop astrologers. So let's look at these first.

Pop Astrologers

In truth, these are usually little more than journalists or show business personalities working on a few vague astrological principles to provide mass predictions of a general and superficial kind. When acting in this capacity, they are in the business of entertainment, not astrology, although sadly many if not most people associate the subject with this kind of razzmatazz.

By necessity, no account can be taken of individual character when such predictions are made. The entire population is divided into twelve groups simply by virtue of whichever part of the year their birthdays happened to occur, (for example, Aries: 21 March – 20 April). This is, of course, regardless of time, or place, or actual year of birth, which, as we have seen, are all vital pieces of information in the composition of a proper natal chart. Fortunately most of us would not act on any of the pronouncements made in articles or programmes of this nature, nor are we intended to. They are there for amusement only, or to fill up a few spare column inches for the editors, and that's all.

It has to be said, however, that many a serious astrologer will supplement or enhance his or her income from the occasional foray into Sun-sign journalism – and it is possible that this trend has actually led to a certain improvement in the quality of much of the popularist stuff in recent times. There is quite a difference now between the best and the worst – although the best is still pretty bad.

The Small Business Person

With the advent of computer technology, it was perhaps inevitable that sooner or later the small business person would stand up and be counted in the astrological world. These are individuals who may well call themselves astrologers when they advertise for your attention in magazines or on the internet – but this is rather like your local pharmacist calling himself a doctor of medicine. These people are in business for business sake, and they work quickly, using computers for interpretation as well as calculation. The kinds of computer programs they have access to vary greatly in sophistication, and of course much depends on the kind of prices quoted in the advertisements, 'You pays your money, you takes your choice'. The results, however, are usually lengthy and ponderous computer print-outs of personality traits which are not always easy reading, being full of contradictions and repetitions.

Using whatever birth data you can supply, complete or otherwise, operators of this kind will run off an analysis of your character, perhaps with a rudimentary forecast attached, for a fee corresponding to about five per cent of the national average weekly wage, or sometimes even less. In recent years, as computers have become faster, prices have come down dramatically. And although the more up-market versions of these packages can provide the newcomer to astrology with an adequate introduction to the subject, they have little real intrinsic value. The whole thing is conducted on a strictly mail order, or

R.S.P.

e-mail basis with no personal contact whatsoever between astrologer and client. Individual factors such as health, environment, relationships and personal aspirations can therefore never be taken into account – and work of this kind is unable to synthesise the various parts of the chart into anything resembling a meaningful whole. Repetitions and contradictions clutter the pages, often leaving the customer feeling dissatisfied or confused. He or she may even feel, not without justification, that they have been taken for a ride.

In this context, beware of advertisements that state categorically that the astrologer does not use computers, does everything by hand on a 'personal basis' and yet still charges you

47

only a few pounds or dollars for the privilege. Remember that genuine astrological work requires hours not minutes to do properly. Consequently, these people are either eccentric millionaires who don't need to earn a living from their astrological services, or they are liars. You decide which before parting with your hard-earned cash.

Private, Semi-professional Astrologers

If value for money is related to the amount of time a fellow human being is prepared to work on your behalf for a limited financial reward, then the men and women in this category are worthy indeed. Invariably, they will have studied astrology over a long period of time, either privately or with one of the principal schools and they will be signatories to a code of ethics, an example of which is reproduced on page 49 in Figure 5. They might advertise their services but usually rely on word-of-mouth recommendations. They are also often to be found through the consultants' lists circulated by the schools.

These are men and women of high integrity who take a sincere pleasure and pride in their work. They will insist on having full and unambiguous birth data to work with, will interpret each client's chart on an individual basis, and will explain their findings carefully and patiently, either in written replies or personally through an informal discussion of the chart itself. Alternatively, the client will be supplied with a cassette recording – either made during the consultation, or separately as an alternative to a written analysis. Computers are used for calculation purposes only. The rest is down to the careful examination and synthesis of all the many variables which, as we have seen, is essential for proper astrological work. A typical assignment of this kind, such as drawing up a natal chart with interpretation and a general forecast for, say, the year ahead, will require one or two days' hard work, therefore, and so fees ranging from about one quarter to one third of the average weekly wage will be quoted. This is actually low-paid work for the number of hours put in, and some additional means of income is sometimes needed.

Astrologers of this kind will often have their own distinct field of expertise and bring their own individual slant to the work that they do, specialising in counselling, for example, or

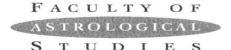

Code of Ethics

Signed by all Diploma holders of the Faculty of Astrological Studies

I accept without reservation the conditions and propositions set out here, and undertake to fulfil these to the best of my ability:

1. I will endeavour to act at all times in such a way as to enhance the good name of astrology, explaining its true nature as I understand it to all interested persons and defending it against unjust aspersions or ill-informed attacks.

2. I will similarly seek to promote the welfare and good name of the Faculty of Astrological Studies by all appropriate and honourable means.

3. I undertake not to use my Diploma qualification in connection with 'sun sign' forecasting for the media.

4. In all my astrological work, whether professional or otherwise, I will abide by the following rules:

    *   When undertaking natal work I will explain clearly that unless the time and place of birth can be given with reasonable accuracy any interpretation supplied must be regarded as incomplete or inadequate.

    *   For all professional work I will charge an adequate fee except in the case of a client who is in genuine need of help but is unable to pay, in which case I will adjust or waive my fee.

    *   I will make an individual and original study of each case, and will not use any form of duplication; nor will I use the writings of others without due acknowledgement. If a computer analysis forms all or part of my work, I will advise the client in advance, and will give a clear explanation of how it differs from an individual non-computerised analysis.

    *   In work stated to be astrological I will not insert anything that is not founded on astrological symbolism. Should I wish to give advice or information derived from other sources, I will do this separately, making clear to the client that it is not based on astrology.

    *   I agree to respect strictly all confidences made to me.

    *   I will not use for my own advantage any knowledge of others gained in the course of my work; nor will I keep for private gain any discoveries I might make which could benefit astrologers generally.

    *   I will use discretion in making any public statement regarding political matters or persons prominent in public life, and will avoid all such as are contrary to good taste or undesirable in the public interest.

Finally, I admit the right of the Council of the Faculty in the event of wilful or grave violation of this Code of Ethics to withdraw my Diploma and erase my name from the Register of Diploma Holders of the Faculty.

Name: .... **Signature:** ....

Date: ....

Figure 5. The Code of Ethics of the Faculty of Astrological Studies

49

providing insights into relationships, or business affairs. Those who go on to become fully professional astrologers will have often served their apprenticeship in this capacity until they have built up a sufficiently large clientele and a good enough track record to be able to rely solely on astrology for an income. Once this is achieved, our dedicated astrologer, for he or she will be dedicated indeed if he is able to reach such a level, will be ready to graduate into our next and final category: the fully fledged professional, earning, we sincerely hope, a comfortable living at his or her craft.

Fully Professional Consultants

These people rarely if ever advertise. They may be qualified through one of the recognised schools, but may also have been taught privately by other astrologers and may, again, specialise in particular fields such as natal, horary or financial astrology, in which they will have great experience and expertise. Naturally, they will command high fees: anything from around half to several times the average weekly wage for a natal chart alone. Their clients will invariably be wealthy and highly successful professional people or representatives of private institutions. Astrologers of this kind will often combine astrology with a further recognised profession such as psychotherapy or investment analysis. The demands of discretion and trust placed upon this type of individual are considerable.

In practice there is no clear-cut distinction between those in the last two categories – semi-professional and fully professional consultants. One tends to evolve into the other, and often the best astrologers are not the ones that command the highest fees. Also, occasionally, an astrologer from the first category – pop astrologers – will be so well-known and so much in demand as to be able to work as a fully professional consultant anyway – and might even have begun their careers in this capacity. As in all walks of life, and all professions, people strive for the highest income possible and so the boundaries often become blurred.

Down to Business – A User's Guide

We have seen that in order to calculate and draw up a suitable birth chart, the exact time, place and date of birth are required.

Therefore, when you contact a semi- or fully professional astrologer, the first thing he or she will want to know is your birth time. If you do not know your exact birth time, the astrologer will probably have one or two useful suggestions as to how this can be ascertained – using a process called rectification, for example, in which past events are used to identify the most likely time of birth.

The next question the astrologer will probably ask is why you want the work done. What exactly are you looking for? This is because most people when they go to an astrologer for the first time are not aware of the variety of jobs that can be undertaken. For example, astrology is not only about forecasting. Many astrologers will confine themselves to character analysis alone. They examine the psychological implications of the birth chart in great detail, the 'personal mythology' of each client, and avoid the area of prediction altogether, believing this to be too unreliable, and believing also that character itself is destiny, and something that shapes our future, anyway.

At the great temple of Apollo at Delphi in classical Greece was to be found the following simple inscription, 'Know thyself'. The ideal in natal astrology is to help people to do just that, to get to know themselves better and thereby encourage each individual to take charge of the present as well as the future. Certainly astrology and counselling blend well in this way, and they are often combined with great success.

Most people, however, are interested in forecasting. They want to know the future trends in their lives, not because they are fatalistic or lazy, but so they can plan for the more positive changes that could be forthcoming, or attempt to steer a path through the negative phases when they, too, come along. Although the birth chart is still the fundamental tool in this respect, predictive work itself is a complex business, and involves far more activity on the part of the astrologer than we have seen so far. For example, one method of forecasting is based on projections of current daily movements of planets (including Sun and Moon) on to natal positions. These are called 'transits to the birth chart'. In other words the astrologer must see whether any planetary movements for, say, the year ahead will make cross aspects to positions in the individual's birth chart.

An example of a transit to a birth chart is shown in Figure 6.

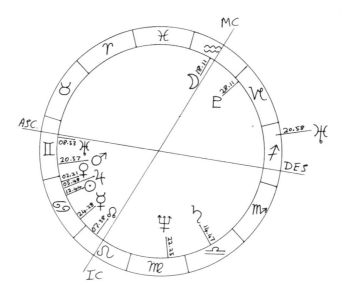

Figure 6. One method of forecasting follows the daily movement of the planets, or 'transits', and relates these to the birth chart. This is a typical example showing transits to such a chart

The birth chart positions are marked inside the chart wheel, while the transiting position for just one planet, Uranus, is drawn on the outside. The most salient cross aspect that Uranus makes on this day is the opposition (180-degree separation) to birth-chart Mars. Mars, as we have seen, is the warrior of the zodiac: aggression, libido, the conquering spirit. Uranus is much less specialised, however: raw energy, chaos and revolution, related to 'the starry sky' in mythology. Its nature is particularly explosive, violent and unpredictable. As it is an outer planet in our solar system, and therefore a slow-moving body as seen from the Earth, this particular aspect can take place only every 84 years. As the opposition of planets is traditionally associated with tension and conflict, one might well expect this to coincide with a rare and unpleasant event.

In fact, the birth chart in this case is not that of a person, but of a nation, the USA, based on the time of the declaration of independence in 1776. The position of Uranus, meanwhile, was for the morning of 28 January 1986, and the launch of the first ill-fated space shuttle, *Challenger*, in which the entire crew perished shortly after take-off. Dedicated to the furthering of 'star wars', the shuttle mission was a national tragedy, which grounded the entire American space programme overnight. Transits can be powerful.

Of course, there are around thirteen fixed points to consider in the natal chart, and at least ten transiting bodies in constant motion every day. Not only transits, but also eclipses are used in this respect. Some astrologers even use the mid-points between the planets, and aspects to these mid-points, making for literally thousands of possible permutations into the future. This is where the skill and experience of the astrologer comes in, knowing which aspects to reject as much as which ones to accept for the purposes of forecasting.

Progressions

Perhaps the most widespread method of forecasting uses the 'progressed chart'. This is a separate chart drawn up for each consecutive day after birth, which in turn corresponds to each consecutive year of life in real terms. In other words, one complete revolution of the Earth on its axis is equated to one revolution of the Earth around the Sun. This day-for-a-year system, as it is sometimes termed, is arguably the practitioner's most valuable tool in predictive work. Again, the astrologer is looking for cross aspects to the birth chart. If, for example, Jupiter were in conjunction with the birth-chart Sun on the thirtieth day after birth, then one would expect the thirtieth year of life to be coloured by that feature. It might mean, among many other possibilities, a prolonged period of study or intellectual expansion, or a long journey.

In practice, the progressed positions are often superimposed on to a copy of the birth chart, usually drawn in a different colour, in order to present this to the client in a more agreeable form. Mutual aspects between bodies within the progressed chart itself are also considered. Meanwhile, the actual interpretation can be presented in a variety of ways. Some astrologers stick to written work, others like to meet with the potential customer first before deciding on the best possible approach to his or her particular enquiry. Still others like to provide the client with a recording of the interview or counselling session. A lot of work can now also be done via e-mail, of course. More than anything though, a good astrologer will always take time to listen to what the client has to say, and will tailor the finished work specifically to that individual's needs and temperament.

You will often be invited into the office of the astrologer so that the qualities, positive and negative, of the chart can be discussed. The tone is invariably friendly and informal, but with frankness and honesty very much to the fore. A client should never expect flattery from any astrologer. That would be a waste of time for all concerned. You will, however, have plenty of opportunity to explain your personal circumstances and your aims and ambitions. As with many other forms of professional guidance, this can prove a highly stimulating and rewarding experience. That one visit, perhaps accompanied by some written work, may well be all you need, but many clients will return for regular meetings and updates, when more specialised work can be undertaken.

Synastry

It is perhaps not generally realised the extent to which astrology can address itself to the often thorny subject of relationships. This is achieved through the comparison of two or more separate birth charts. Again, it is a case of looking for cross aspects, but this time between bodies in one birth chart and another. By this, one can judge compatibility, shared interests, points of conflict, and so on. This kind of astrology is called synastry (*syn* = together; *astra* = star).

In a romantic relationship, for instance, one is looking for connections between the Sun, Moon, Mars and Venus, cross aspects from one birth chart to another. One partner might have, say, the Sun in a square (90-degree) aspect to the other's Moon; or Venus to the other's Mars, and so on. Again, there are many possible permutations, particularly if all the other planets are compared one to the other in this way. Taken together, the otherwise bewildering range of human relationships and interactions can be understood at least to some extent through work of this kind and, perhaps equally as importantly, discussed and pondered over by those involved.

Horary

Undergoing something of a revival in recent years, the branch of astrology called horary (Latin 'of the hour') deals with the answering of specific questions, and in the hands of a skilled and experienced practitioner can throw up some truly remarkable conclusions. The birth data of the individual concerned is not normally used. Instead a chart is drawn up for the moment the question is asked, the 'birth' of the question, and judged accordingly. The theory underlying horary is that if any given moment in time contains a question, then it must also contain the answer, if only we are clever enough to be able to perceive it. Horary is one excellent tool for assisting this process. It should be remembered, however, that accuracy can only be achieved when the client is sincere in their approach, and clear on the information he or she wishes to obtain, and can therefore formulate a precise and lucid question to work with.

There are many well-documented cases in which horary charting has produced spectacular results. In the UK, the late Oliver Barclay, founder of an excellent distance-learning program for those wanting to study the traditional techniques of horary astrology, used to have an uncanny knack of being able to locate lost animals or pets using the tenets of horary astrology. The owner, who might for example have lost his pet cat, would simply phone and ask, 'Where is Tiddles?' Immediately a chart would be drawn up for that precise moment so that information could be deduced as to the likely direction, surrounds and conditions in which the animal will be located. That's horary astrology. And it works!

Financial Astrology

The hard-nosed world of big business also occasionally takes more than a passing interest in astrology. Astrology has always been employed in the drawing up of what are called electional charts. These are used for determining the most suitable times for embarking on a business venture, signing a contract, or even the laying of a foundation stone. This kind of astrology is still widespread in the East – while in the West, astrologers are far more likely to be employed in speculating on economic trends and the fluctuations of stock market and commodity prices. The 'first trade' chart of a company, when it is first floated on the stock exchange, forms a valid tool for investigation and speculation. It is part of a vast array of tools that comprise the body of knowledge termed 'technical analysis'.

Every major financial company, bank and commodity firm has among its full-time staff people engaged in technical analysis. These may or may not be interested in astrology, but most will be at least aware of it, and its potential as a possible contributing factor in the feverish world of stock market prediction. There are many, many tools available to the technical analyst, but astrology is certainly one which can be, and is used. It is a practice far more wide-spread than many would realise, so that it is possibly open to question now to what extent astrological counselling foresees or actually contributes to certain shifts in trading sentiment. It is sometimes difficult to disentangle the two, because all of the world's great financial centres, London, New York, Tokyo and Hong Kong, have their financial astrologers, whose work must by necessity remain secret much of the time.

Astrology and Academia

As you can see, there is plenty of variety and plenty of choice within the profession. But outside of this you will also find many interested amateurs and serious students of astrology. And now once again, after a pause of some centuries, astrology is also the subject of legitimate academic study. In 2002 an MA in the critical study of Cultural Astronomy and Astrology commenced at Bath Spa University College, plus additional modules on astrology included in university courses elsewhere in the UK. In the USA there is the Kepler College offering a four-year BA program, and also a two-year Associate of Arts Degree in the history and symbolism of astrology.

In addition to these exciting developments, there are numerous smaller, more specialised schools – such as The Faculty of Astrological Studies and the Mayo School in the UK and the American Federation of Astrologers in the US. And of course the subject has long been taught locally at adult education level in most countries in the West. Some useful addresses and websites are listed at the end of the book for those who might be interested in studying the subject in this way with the back-up and support of dedicated teachers and staff.

I hope all this has by now gone some way towards answering the question: What is Astrology? It is a question that is always going to be hard to answer because there is hardly a facet of life that it does not embrace. The arts, sciences, social and political institutions, families, businesses, nations, all are accessible and open to investigation. It is above all else a practical and useful pursuit, providing guidance, information, and an especially creative and dynamic vehicle for self-discovery.

What astrology is not, however, and this might well surprise many of its critics, is fatalistic or dogmatic. At the core of all genuine astrological work, particularly in the twentieth century, is the recognition of free will and self-determination as fundamental facts of life. Like the American Constitution, 'We hold these truths to be self-evident': independence, liberty and the pursuit of happiness. In truth, astrologers and their adherents have nearly always considered the higher or 'thinking' part of the human being to be absolutely free. Only the lower self, the body, the passions and the senses are subject to natural forces. Whether the stars and planets contain the origins of such natural forces, or whether they are simply indicators of a process common to all, is of little real consequence. The two happen together, that's all; and changes inside of us are synchronised with changes in the heavens. This is altogether a highly convenient state of affairs and it seems only sensible to take advantage.

Astrology is one rather good way of providing information, therefore, one more valuable string to the bow. Used intelligently it can be of inestimable value in negotiating a course through the turbulent world of human affairs. Astrology is there to be used.

When you go to your friendly neighbourhood astrologer, therefore, do not expect him or her to provide concrete directives for conducting your future. Do not expect a list of the inescapable calamities and golden moments of good fortune that must surely wait in your predestined future. If your astrologer is any good at his or her job, such an approach will never be considered. The astrologer is not a crystal gazer, not a clairvoyant, not a magician. He or she is interested only in facts, and in how these can relate to your existence in the here and now. The astrologer believes that what you become tomorrow is largely a result of how you see yourself today. You will be helped to see yourself accurately. The rest is up to you.

Now having well and truly nailed our colours to the mast it is time to consider matters of survival. Self-defence for astrology and astrologers. Read on.

PART TWO

Self-defence

CHAPTER 5

Dealing with the Bully
– or what to do before the doctor calls

No matter if professional, amateur or simply an ardent enthusiast of astrology, each of us is likely to encounter a certain animosity from time to time. Even those with just a passing interest in the subject can feel intimidated. Why should we astrologers put up with this? Why so often, whether in a social situation, with family and friends, or in our day-to-day routine among colleagues and work mates, do we passively accept a reaction from others which, when unfavourable, can range from silent indifference to utter horror and indignation. All this simply because we have, perhaps inadvertently, perhaps on purpose, let it be known that we sympathise with the fundamental astrological tenet that the movements of the Sun, Moon and planets, together with the spatial co-ordinates of horizon and zodiac, have some form of correspondence with the lives of individual people here on Earth. Seems reasonable enough!

Just suppose that someone has posed one of those ubiquitous social questions, 'What do you do? What are your interests or hobbies? What sort of things do you like reading?'

When the time comes for us to reply we shouldn't balk at it. We should be confident that we can back up our position, that we can relax and enjoy the conversation – to explain ideas if possible, or defend ourselves and resist abuse if necessary. In short, it's about time we started sticking up for ourselves.

Firstly, let us assume that any attack we are likely to experience will be basically verbal in nature. Thus, you might be relieved to know, this book stops well short of the point where you will be urged to roll up your sleeves and resort to fisticuffs! Nevertheless, it is worth remembering that what holds good for a physical contest often proves relevant in debate. Many experts in the field of self-defence would probably agree that the ancient Chinese system of tai chi ch'uan remains one of supreme forms of martial art. Paradoxically, however, one of the most interesting aspects of tai chi is that it is also often taught as a means of relaxation and of staying fit and well. And, indeed, to see tai chi being practised is rather like observing a wholly natural process: a graceful slow-motion 'dance', featuring remarkably soft and delicate movements – called, in tai chi, a 'form'. Regular practice of the form helps to develop a unique combination of vitality, concentration and, most important, inner calm. When this is blended with the strength and experience of the tai chi master and applied to the purpose of self-defence the outcome is formidable, indeed. Trying to overpower such a person is like trying to catch a shadow or grasp the wind. This should be our inspiration and our guiding principle in our efforts to defend astrology – that is, knowing the arguments fully and then cultivating sufficient calm and self-confidence to be able to react effectively when challenged.

Posture and Attitude

The first law of self-defence, in tai chi or anywhere else – physical or verbal – is *be aware*. Treating everyone as a potential aggressor might seem to be a little paranoid, but it need not be so. There is absolutely no need to be tense or withdrawn. Simply be aware that even the most friendly and amicable of individuals can turn exceptionally nasty at the slightest mention of the word astrology. This normally arises from a deep-seated fear of the irrational and, therefore, of the unconscious – be it his or her own unconscious or the seemingly often-violent unconscious promptings of others. They are anxious, therefore, because you are forcing them to think and to delve into what for them could be a murky and infrequently visited part of their psyche – the imagination.

This part of the book, self-defence, ranges from the most basic, often trivial assaults right through to debate at a high level of understanding. We are going to approach these levels by degrees. Initially, therefore, we need to equip ourselves with a few basic blocks or defensive postures, simple things we can deploy at short notice during any sudden, unprovoked moment of aggression. Bear in mind that these are not designed to be devastating, but simply to check your opponent's progress. They will give you time, a vital breathing space in which to prepare a more penetrating counter-attack or to develop a proper debate by mustering some of your more heavyweight arguments, examples of which will be introduced later in this book. Remember, the 'bully' is a crude kind of beast, and will almost certainly not have prepared an offensive. If you have at least mastered the correct posture, you already have the advantage. In this, there are a few basic rules that must be observed.

To begin with, as in any normal day-to-day situation, you should appear open, relaxed and accessible. Look your opponent straight in the eye, especially when he or she is talking. If tensions are running high, fix your gaze just between the eyes. Try to keep an open, relaxed stance, and avoid fidgeting or grinning too much. This may sound trite, but remember many people will expect you, as an enthusiast of astrology, to be a bit eccentric anyway, and they will already be looking out for odd little traits and mannerisms to confirm their suspicions. Fidgeting nervously might be one of them. Don't go there! And for the gentlemen: you should be aware that having your hands in your pockets is also a rather secretive and furtive-looking position. People like to see your hands. If you are wearing a jacket, keep it unbuttoned. A buttoned-up chest gives the impression of someone closed in and resisting intimacy.

If the exchange is on an equable, polite level you may retain this open stance. If the confrontation becomes offensive, however, you can start to introduce some rejection postures: legs and arms crossed; hands hidden, just up behind the neck if seated, or behind the back if standing. Searching for something in your jacket, briefcase or handbag, or fixing your eyes on something happening at the other side of the room, are all effective ways of detaching yourself from the conversation. Turning your head away while someone is speaking can also have a most disconcerting effect. But remember, it is not a matter of proving that you are right, or of appearing superior. None of that is important at this stage. And the moment you feel you are becoming emotionally involved, feeling threatened in any sense by someone's unreasonable aggression, remove yourself physically from the scene – and quickly. In any event, it should certainly be beneath your dignity to indulge in a slanging match. The great Chinese classic, the *Tao Te Ching*, has something interesting to say on this topic:

'He who knows does not speak;
He who speaks does not know.
He who is truthful is not showy;
He who is showy is not truthful.
He who is virtuous does not dispute;
He who disputes is not virtuous.'[1]

Know the Enemy

Consider, for a moment, these two statements, made by two hypothetical people:

1) I am a cynic. I like practical jokes and having fun. I don't like being told what to do, and I don't take anything in life seriously. That way nobody can criticise me or hurt me, like they once did when I was small.

2) I have faith in a meaningful universe. I enjoy exploring the world of the unseen, and I like doing astrology. I know I might be putting my head above the parapet, occasionally, when I do this. But I am not frightened.

These two individuals and their views encapsulate the situation in which you will often find yourself. The first person here is, of course, your opponent. The second is yourself. Never lose sight of this simple distinction, which will almost always have some validity.

Elements

Of course, in the rough-and-tumble of real-life debate, things are never quite that simple. And for our purposes in this chapter it is also going to be helpful to view the 'enemy' as belonging to one of four main types of personality corresponding to the four elements of astrology: Fire, Earth, Air and Water. Part of your initial training should be to try, as quickly as possible, whenever you encounter a stranger or are introduced to anyone for the first time, to form an opinion of his or her element. This may not necessarily correspond with their Sun sign, of course. The element-balance of an individual reflects the 'whole' person in a way the Sun sign can never do. The Chinese and those in the West practising acupuncture, homeopathy, etc. still use this form of judgement in the diagnosis of illnesses, as did the old European physicians, of course, with their four humours:

Choleric, Melancholic, Sanguine and Phlegmatic. Some psychologists, especially those who adhere to the Jungian scheme of things, also make use of what are called the four functions of consciousness: Intuition, Sensation, Thinking and Feeling. Similar stuff.

For those not familiar with this time-honoured approach to evaluating personality and individual temperament, the following table might be helpful. The various systems just mentioned are co-ordinated under the astrological elements. Study this for a while; read through the following paragraphs, then go out and do a little bit of 'people-watching' for yourself and you will be surprised at how quickly you can become skilled at observing and understanding the world in this way. It can be useful.

Element	Humour	Type
Fire	Choleric	Intuition
Earth	Melancholic	Sensation
Air	Sanguine	Thinking
Water	Phlegmatic	Feeling

Note: Phlegmatic can also be applied to Earth, as can Melancholic to Water. They are interchangeable.

Defence Postures

Let's examine each element in turn and take a look also at some basic defence postures that may be used against each type – simple evasions, parries or cut-off remarks designed to neutralise the bully or to finish the exchange quickly. These are listed according to the element type against which they are the most effective – though you can easily swap them around, of course, and adapt them to your own situation if and when it changes. They will stand you in good stead later when you come to sparring and, ultimately, real combat situations, so study them carefully.

Fire

You will easily spot the Fire types. They are hard to ignore. When they attack, it may often be unprovoked: aggressive, direct, full steam ahead – a bluster of a sentence such as, 'You don't believe in all that junk, do you?' Very succinct and to the point, Fire people.

This type, the life and soul of the party, appears confident and yet dreads that their popularity might ever flag. Some appear to be on a personal crusade against what they see as darkness and ignorance – anything that in the least antagonises or threatens the comfortable and cosy world in which they feel dominant. This type also loves to hand out tips and advice, and loves to be thought of as up-to-date, practical and informed.

Watch out for the confident, even arrogant Fire type, the pouting Lions, the zealous Rams. Watch out for the studied flamboyance, the loud voice, those who seem to have an opinion on just about anything. Be prepared, too, for the most outrageous remarks of all from those Sagittarians, who will delight in the most clumsy and ill-timed observations on anything from your political ideology to the colour of your socks.

By all appearances the most formidable, the Fire type is in fact the easiest to keep at arm's length. It's mostly all bluff and bravado when they attack – while you, on the other hand, will be ready to respond with some direct blocks and counter-moves. In the meantime, keep up the banter, and keep it simple. Your opponents will soon have wasted a lot of energy, as well as all their best gags, and probably have attracted a fair degree of unwelcome attention from other people nearby in any social situation.

Keep hands linked behind your back in a control posture. You are not in the least bit impressed and are not having any of it. If you are seated during any of this, try an upward arm stretch whilst reclining. Yawn or communicate sympathy or feelings of tedium while gazing at others in their company. They are almost certainly as bored as you are by all the histrionics. You may even get onlookers on your side by making the odd joke at your opponent's expense.

Actually, Fire types at their best are if nothing else usually forthright and open, and like to think of themselves as honest too. So, if your antagonist is not being too objectionable, simply use this word 'honest' in a quick cut-off remark – something like:

'Let's be honest, there's not much point in you and I talking about this subject, is there?' This will often work immediately. Peace returns.

Meanwhile, and especially in a social situation, the more purely aggressive, usually inebriated individual can be safely allowed to continue, plunging further and further into more and more advanced states of desperation until even they realise they have gone too far. You can then laugh it off and turn your attention to other things, perhaps delivering a quick sideways thrust at the same time, such as:

'Excuse me, would you mind just moving your charisma a little to one side so I can see if there's anything else going on over there.'

People in the group will probably be so embarrassed by your opponent's poor behaviour by this time that the enemy will become completely isolated, and might even skulk away to lick their wounds elsewhere. He or she is not likely to want to speak to you again, incidentally, so you will have no further bother.

Earth

The stodgy, unimaginative Earth type could well be the most common adversary you will encounter. This is never an easy kind to defend against, because the attack often takes place quietly when your back is turned. Although contrary to his or her own self-image, the Earth type is prone, when excited or threatened, to give way to all kinds of irrational fears and to reach instantly for the panacea of dogma and orthodoxy. Life, for them, is keeping strictly to the routine of working, eating, sleeping and so on. They are the people who have got things 'just about right' while anyone who wastes time on non-profit making work or mental exploration of any sort, is a fool.

Do not always expect a courteous exchange of views therefore. This type will grunt its disapproval, shrug its shoulders or simply ignore you altogether. This is also the 'rock', the 'real man', who is terrified of ever appearing vulnerable or eccentric. Their practicality and realism can be impervious. In social terms, the fear is of rejection by the group, and hence deprivation. The material, often greedy, nature of the Earth type lives in dread of this.

All this may sound bad enough, but if you are ever unfortunate enough to encounter one of the really stroppy Earth types that dislikes just about everything in life that can't be eaten, you will have to be especially careful. The very proximity of an astrologer can bring out all the negative characteristics of this otherwise excellent element. Be prepared for anger, indignation, obstinacy: an aggressive verbal charge from the Taurean bull or

Capricorn goat that could knock you completely off balance.

Humour and wit should be employed, as well as a certain nonchalance. Don't let yourself appear too concerned. This is especially valuable in a social situation, as it threatens your opponent with a sense of alienation. At all times remain respectful. Keep your head erect and, if seated, your hands together, fingers pointed. This creates the impression of calm self-confidence. It is also the pose of the specialist or expert, or of the teacher in the face of a quarrelsome child. It threatens a kind of parental disapproval and subsequently – most dreadful of all to Earth types, remember – deprivation. When confronted directly, try a quick side step such as:

'Astrology, of course, doesn't have all the answers. It requires an open mind.'

Here you are touching the raw nerve of the Earth type: complacency. This will usually work, but it could, in rare circumstances be inflammatory. If the genuinely disgruntled Earth type appears to be squaring up for a real onslaught, often voiced in the form of a grunt or a snort or two, respond with a rapid body swerve such as:

'I think we can at least agree that there is no point in coming to blows over it, don't you?'

He or she will, in fact, probably quieten down instantly and agree that this sounds reasonable enough. Earth types do respect reason. But if not … *run*.

Air

The Air type, if anti-astrology, is the one most likely to view the subject as an insult to his or her intelligence. Air people believe in the power of the brain, and of logic, but they may not be sufficiently aware of the full range of astrology in the light of modern research and practice to be much impressed. And although some Air types could well be absorbed in the study of related subjects such as psychology, complementary medicine, etc., they may still be reluctant to express any kind of visible commitment. Alternatively, they may already have a degree of knowledge and be stimulated by the mythology and history of astrology, but – again – they prefer to keep this interest at arm's length, thus ultimately rejecting something they might dearly like to believe in. Many astronomers fall into this mould.

These intellectual, loquacious individuals are often a pleasure to deal with and actually the type most open to debate and polite argument – that is of course provided he or she is in a good mood. Needing to remain logical and reasonable at all times, and finding the world of feelings rather incomprehensible and fraught with danger, they will usually want to keep things on a rational footing. Their challenges are likely to be mild and edged with curiosity, though the bully among this type could be sarcastic as well.

Keep a direct and steady gaze and, if seated, allow the occasional gesture of attentiveness to appear, letting the fingers grip the chin, or tilting the head slightly to one side. Show respect for the other's intelligence, but make it obvious that you consider yourself their equal, and be ready to respond with a few well-placed examples of astrology's uses, concentrating on practical results, even some statistics (the kind of thing you will find later in this book). These will at least elevate the contest to a more dignified level.

Occasionally, though, you may cross swords with a more superficial type – the clever and mercurial Gemini at its worst and most shallow. These are harder to handle, and if really psyched-up, the satirical Air type can simply disintegrate an opponent under a laser-sharp beam of wit and cynicism. Much of this will be swift, genuinely brilliant and in fact quite funny. In a social situation, you can expect to be the brunt of numerous gibes and wisecracks. Watch for the barrage of words, the quick repartee. This could even be quite cruel and offensive, and you will have to be sharp to keep ahead.

Your best line of defence, if it is a genuinely witty attack, is to laugh along with it. Don't hold yourself in or appear to take yourself too seriously. This type takes *nothing* seriously and has a way of making stiffness and formality look ridiculous. Keep your head erect, and foster a slightly ironic gaze. If seated, let your hands drift behind your head occasionally, as though you are enjoying it all immensely. Then, once your opponent has rolled off a particularly corny or hackneyed remark, respond with a good swift jab such as:

'If I were you I'd put that one back in the Christmas cracker where you found it.'

This may well hit a soft spot, since Air types like to see themselves as original and clever. Your remark makes their humour look rather stale, and you are now back in control of the situation. Alternatively, you can express a willingness to discuss the subject in a more sober fashion, in a spirit of courtesy. That might change things around – but otherwise it is best to remove yourself from the vicinity. If they call after you, just smile and hold your hand to your ear as you go. You didn't quite catch what they said, and you have lost interest now anyway.

Water

Generally, the 'feeling' type of person typified by the Water element is likely to be sympathetic to the metaphysical or mystical dimension of life. But remember we are interested here only in the version that could prove a potential aggressor, the kind that has had his or her emotional being distorted by painful experience. Water-element people have deep feelings; and when they hurt, they hurt badly. In consequence, they are likely to prove the most passionate cynics and sceptics of all. Here you find the bitter Scorpions and Crabs; the totally detached Fishes.

They do like to probe, however, to grub around beneath the surface, to expose all those old wives' tales or follies. You can hear them in conversation exploding myths or debunking popular heroic reputations in the way other people might be cracking walnuts.

Example: 'Oh, of course Francis Drake wasn't playing bowls at all when the news of the Armada came. He was actually in bed asleep – ha, ha! And the only reason we won anyway was because of the appalling English weather.'

Example: 'Well, naturally, the whole motivation behind space exploration is purely military. Romantic notions aside, it all comes down to getting a useful return for your money.'

And in between such startling revelations as these you may well detect something like, 'Naturally, anyone with any sense realises there is absolutely no rational or scientific evidence for ESP, divination, astrology or any of those other attractive superstitions.'

You might notice here that the enemy could be fairly articulate, perhaps even quite an academic. But do not forget the earlier point that your presence is always likely to tweak at the hidden nerve of repressed feelings. The rationality which, by way of compensation, they strive for so fervently and yet usually stumble over so heavily when put to the test, is likely to desert them at precisely such moments – as if they are fighting for their lives to prove you wrong. Indeed, in some cases they may be doing just that. Feelings can literally kill the moody Water type.

Look out, too, for the other, less lucid variants: the disgruntled nine-to-five worker, for example. The discovery that you are earning a living, or even a little pocket money, doing something you clearly enjoy could be bitterly resented by anyone stuck in a rut. Watch out for the simmering gaze across a crowded room while he or she eavesdrops on your conversation. And although you can attempt to draw the more genteel types into a discussion, remember that in eyeball-to-eyeball conversation with Water people it is always advisable to be prepared for the worst, which can be vicious irony and cynicism. He or, more rarely she, is basically a person who does not wish to be seen to yield. They were once idealists before disappointments and misfortune turned them in on themselves – and nothing is more unreasonable than a frustrated idealist. When repressed feelings are on the line, the Water types can become hysterical in their criticism. A simple defensive block on your part could in rare circumstances spark off a vicious counter-attack that could be tearful or even downright brutal.

If standing, cross the arms. This is a 'shutting-out' gesture. Look sympathetically but distantly upon their ravings. Use a gentle warding-off manoeuvre, such as:

'I'm sorry to see that this subject upsets you so much.'

This is likely either to throw them entirely off balance or else initiate a swift counter-thrust to the effect of how utterly unconcerned they are. You can deflect this easily with a look or expression of disbelief.

Worried that they are giving away too much, exposing too many feelings, they will probably retreat. Make a pact with them not to drag emotion into the argument. You remain always the person of reason, therefore.

There is another equally effective way to deal with the situation, which may be less painful for your opponent. This is simply to show your feelings: in fact you can be quite free and unreserved in this. Press back against your antagonist with something like, 'Would you excuse me, please. I find this all rather unnecessary and distressing. I hope you can understand.'

71

And then prepare to make your exit, looking a little saddened by the whole affair.

This will take your opponents aback. It may actually make them feel rather ashamed, and they will not pursue you further, unless to apologise. Strange as it may seem, this is a tactic that can turn an enemy into a friend for life! Water types understand emotion and respect deep feelings. They know how easily it is to be hurt and will regret having made such a bad impression on a stranger.

So much for recognising the bully, who will usually only attack within a social or group situation: showing off. This is their own system of defence too, of course, for, as in all walks of life, the bully is only a coward with a fierce countenance.

Remember, when responding don't waste time considering the nature of your opponent's Sun sign. Simply estimate the element he or she most evinces. Then go for the soft spot, the one most vulnerable to that element. In other words:

Fire – Hit at the vanity.
Earth – Hit at the intransigence.
Air – Hit at the indecisiveness.
Water – Hit at the jealousies and resentments.

Important ... never, under any circumstances, initiate a confrontation. Remember, always, that *you* are the secure one. You do not need to prove anything to anybody. In conversation, never tempt an opening by drawing upon astrology. Never advertise yourself or your interest in this area. Wait until you are asked. Then distinguish between a polite enquiry and a genuine attack. When challenged, meet force with equal force, always by degrees proportional and just a little greater than the force being directed against you and your beliefs. Above all never lose your temper. Treat everyone with politeness, even those who are rude. This is not necessarily because they are good and kind, but because *you* are.

CHAPTER 6

Basic Blocks

By now you should be reasonably well-equipped at dealing with the bully. However, you will eventually need to get to grips with some more evolved arguments, 'basic blocks' that can be used in your own and astrology's defence whenever an intelligent approach is made by an opponent with a genuine point of view. As distinct to the more emotional and superficial confrontations described in the last chapter, the following basic blocks are designed to enable you to resist challenges that refer directly to astrology. They should be learnt well, almost by heart, so that they will emerge spontaneously or at least seemingly without effort. You can then embark upon a more penetrating counter-offensive if necessary, using the more evolved arguments presented later on.

Speed is of the essence, as in any combat scenario, but do not worry if you are initially slow. If you learn the blocks well, they will come out readily and instinctively with practice. This is vital because, if delivered quickly and firmly, a well-placed block can put your opponent totally off balance. For our purposes, and to be truly effective these will need to take the form of a short sentence or two delivered immediately the attacker makes the first real move, without allowing them time to gain the upper hand. Meanwhile, you should already have established the element type you are dealing and will have adopted the relevant defensive posture. Remember the basic rules: arms away from chest, never folded; feet a little apart; don't fidget and grin too much, and look your opponent straight in the eye as often as necessary to make your point.

Typical attacks with suitable defensive statements now follow, and here I shall present two variations of these: firstly, an all-purpose block, one that can be used for general use by just about anyone no matter how slender your commitment to astrology, and secondly a more specialised version, pitched more to the needs of the working astrologer. In time you should be able to adapt and combine these blocks to defend against many different lines of attack.

'An Astrologer! Really, you don't believe in all that stuff, do you?'
All-purpose block: 'Certainly I do. It's helped me on many

occasions to make important decisions ... and to avoid making a fool of myself.'

Specialist block: 'Of course I believe in it! I wouldn't expect to earn a living at something I didn't believe in.'

Note: both these replies demonstrate the free-will emphasis of modern astrology. You are seen as a person of action, someone who puts astrology to constructive use. The all-purpose block also suggests in a subtle way that the opponent might be appearing foolish.

'Astrology! Oh, I always read mine in the newspapers. It never comes true.'

All-purpose block: 'Well, you shouldn't believe all you read in the papers.'

Specialist block: 'I'm not surprised. That's not astrology you're talking about – it's journalism.'

Note: these two can be linked up to form a double block that can be very effective. Judge the ferocity, or otherwise, of the attack and react accordingly.

'Erm ... Actually, I believe people make their own luck.'

All-purpose block: 'That's right; people do make their own luck. And astrology is concerned with what makes people make their own luck.'

Specialist block: 'Yes, the first thing any reputable astrologer would impress on you is the importance of free choice. Astrology is a bit like the weather forecast. The experts can tell you if it's likely to rain or not – but it's up to you to take an umbrella.'

'Hey! This guy's an astrologer!' (in a group situation)

All-purpose block: 'Don't worry, it's not contagious. And it rarely proves fatal.'

Specialist block: 'Yes, I'm fortunate enough to be able to earn a living doing something I thoroughly enjoy.'

Note: both these blocks are a bit cheeky, and can easily unsettle your opponent. But don't feel guilty. This person is, after all, probably trying to unsettle you, at least to begin with. Remember it is essential to remain calm and cheerful when speaking. Don't become snooty.

'*Astrology – really! How extraordinary!*' (the patronising type)
All-purpose block: 'Not really all that extraordinary. Just a rather useful hobby, that's all. One more string to the bow.'
Specialist block: 'Well, we've been around since about 3000 BC. I'd have thought most people would have been used to us by now.'
Note: these present the astrologer in a cheerful ordinary light, a visage which will undoubtedly surprise such an opponent, who probably expects you to have at least two heads and a magic wand tucked under your arm.

'*Astrology! You're not serious, are you? Get real!*'
All-purpose block: 'Well, I'll be serious if you'd like. But I don't think we need to get too uptight about it.'
Specialist block: 'Well, when you spend at times twelve hours a day, five days a week doing something, it's difficult not to take it seriously. It certainly seems real to me! Luckily, it's a particularly interesting job, and also a lot of fun.'
Note: These replies can unsteady your opponent by making them appear rather tedious. Most people prefer someone who is relaxed and with a sense of humour; and so it's not too difficult to gain the upper hand by using these tactics.

'Oh well, yes, I'm sure it works out sometimes, this astrology business. But that's just coincidence in my view.'
Note: Coincidence is a favourite word among cynics who use it almost as a kind of magical incantation to avoid addressing many of life's mysteries.
All-purpose block: 'Calling something a coincidence doesn't explain why it happens. I like to know why things happen, and when they are most likely to happen again.'
Specialist block: 'Yes, it does work out, and frequently. As for coincidence, well, it's just a word that means two things that happen together at the same time: co-incident. The word itself doesn't get us any closer to explaining what takes place. Astrology, on the other hand, is interested in what lies behind the words, the reality of how things relate.'

Your main aim here in any such encounter is to appear more broadminded and thoughtful than your competitor.

'Astrology! Good heavens, surely you must realise ... Do you really not understand the utter impossibility of ...' **(and they will then go on, and on, and on)**

Occasionally you will be unfortunate enough to encounter this kind of 'informed' person who might astonish you by a sudden onslaught of words, a kind of instant vehemence, as though being introduced to an astrologer had suddenly released years of pent-up indignation and resentment. They may bring up the opinions of respected scholars and scientists, their own passionate misgivings on superstition and fatalism: in short everything and anything except astrology itself! Let them have their say, and then ...

All-purpose block: 'Could you just repeat that please while I take notes.'

Specialist block: 'I see. But, do you know anything at all about the profession of astrology? I mean, have you studied the procedure: how it works, where it's applied and what exactly it's used for?'

To which you will receive the inevitable:

'Well no, not really, but ...'

Don't let them continue after the 'but'. Simply nod your head and say, 'Oh, I see.' Then turn slightly to one side, losing complete interest in them. The result can be devastating, and you may need to adjust the level of your indignation a little if you feel your opponent might, after all, become interested in a genuine discussion.

Note: both these answers, in their own way, will show you in a position of self-control and good humour: an ideal state to maintain at this stage of any encounter.

'Astrology ... Oh, well I'm not really all that sure if I believe in stuff like that. Hope you don't mind.'

Here we have the typical indecisive type: the kind who normally has to have their opinions made up for them. Look out for the latest fashions in dress or the folded newspaper under the arm.

All-purpose block: 'Not at all. I'm very broadminded about that sort of thing.'

Specialist block: 'Oh, that's all right. Neither was I until I studied the subject for myself. I gave it a fair trial, and was rather impressed. It was soon after this when I decided to study it in earnest, and make it an important part of my life (or profession).'

Note: the all-purpose block here highlights your antagonist's evident lack of broadmindedness, a fault that you are likely to encounter in almost every opponent. This particular block is well worth learning, therefore, and you can employ it quite freely at any time and in almost any situation.

'Astrology ... no, surely you mean astronomy, don't you? Well, I'm amazed, frankly, that someone like yourself should take that sort of thing seriously.'

Here it is apparent that you have already made a fair impression on your opponent (which is at least encouraging), as he or she is evidently stunned to discover you are concerned with astrology – something with which they probably have little positive experience. This surprise is, naturally, to your advantage and you can force your opponent to trip up quite easily.

All-purpose block: 'Yes, astro' with a logos. That's it. Actually you don't have to commit intellectual suicide to believe in astrology: only take a few risks. You have to be prepared to look afresh at the serious side of the subject. Then I think you'll be impressed. Most people are.'

Specialist block: 'Well, most of my clients are intelligent, honest, professional people, and they certainly take it seriously. Then perhaps they're lucky enough to have been introduced to genuine astrology from the start and realise that the stuff in the newspapers or on TV, which is what you probably have in mind, is not at all representative of the subject.'

'Huh! All that sort of thing is just pure escapism, in my view, a search for mystery and excitement: compensation for people who don't already have anything interesting going on in their lives. That's all there is to astrology and things like that.'

Here is another one of those down-to-earth types who pride themselves on their sense of 'realism'. For them, astrology is inextricably linked with things like Ouija boards, séances and paperbacks on UFOs and the Bermuda Triangle. They are easy to tackle.

All-purpose block: 'So what's wrong with a little mystery and excitement? These are emotional realities that we all need in our lives: sources of inspiration and renewal. Surely you don't believe there can be anything wrong in such valuable and enormously entertaining sensations!'

Specialist block: 'To say that astrology just deals with mystery and excitement is like telling a doctor that he deals only with worry and hypochondria. Astrology is a complete and thorough profession, dealing with ideas, concepts and actions.'

A few quick jabs

You will have noticed so far that our blocks have been mild in nature because dignity and calm are qualities that will usually restrain unwarranted aggression, even when your arguments are below their possible best. Remember, a sharp tongue and a dull mind usually go together. You do not deserve to be thought of in this way, so remain polite.

Having said this, it is sometimes useful to be able to counter-attack with a little more vigour, to put in a few quick jabs to interrupt the thrust of any reproach or attempted rebuttal that comes your way. The knack of knowing when and how to jab and harry your opponent is easily learnt. Listen out for certain key words. If the words 'justify' or 'justice' are used, for example, 'I can't see any justification for astrology,' you respond with something like, 'It's a poor judge who reaches a verdict without knowing all the facts.'

If he or she criticises but won't listen, or tells you they already understand enough to dismiss the subject, you hit back with, 'Surely no one can dismiss something they're not willing to have explained or put to the test', or, 'You may already know enough to sustain your opinions, but is that sufficient to dismiss something with the intellectual range and antiquity of astrology?'

If the word 'pessimism' is used or pessimism expressed about ever finding anything of value in astrology, you come back with, 'True. Pessimists rarely make the discoveries that optimists make, nor have as much fun making them.'

If, after the initial approach, your opponent suddenly turns away stating angrily that it's just a waste of time discussing such nonsense, you should agree, and then counter straight away with, 'There can only be losers all round when reason has to pit itself against emotion.'

In these replies, always stress your opponent's possible prejudgement of the matter. This prejudgement will almost certainly be the case, for – as you will see from the wealth of evidence for the acceptance or at least the sober consideration of astrology that appears later in this book – there are absolutely no excuses for your opponent's disapproval other than varying degrees of ignorance. This is even more the case if he or she is behaving badly. In fact the worse the behaviour, the easier it is for you to reveal and exploit the unsteadiness of their entire stance.

As you will come to realise, both justice and hard evidence are on your side. Two formidable weapons. Use them.

CHAPTER 7

Introducing the Form

We have already dealt adequately with the impolite or sarcastic opponent, and it is assumed from now on that there is real value in pursuing a discussion and presenting a genuine defence of astrology. Your opponent is now able and willing to discuss ideas and exchange opinions rationally and so in the next two chapters we are going to move beyond the simple blocks and parries used in the average social situation, and look towards real discussion and argument: offence and counter-offensive of a reasonably high calibre. In this, as with the higher levels of the martial arts, we should maintain a deep and natural respect for our opponent and avoid all bitterness, resentment and innuendo. For remember, the greatest force operating against astrology today is not hostility – but ignorance. Your task, therefore, is not only to defend but also to reassure and to educate others.

The subject covers such a vast field that we will need a system to help us. Therefore we will explore, one by one, the twelve basic kinds of critique most often targeted against astrology. Collectively, these twelve sections can be viewed as a kind of 'form', a term borrowed from the ancient Chinese art of tai chi ch'uan. The form is used in training, and describes a continuous flow of defensive and counter-offensive moves executed slowly and in a relaxed fashion. In this way, concentration, patience and humility are developed, qualities every bit as important as fighting skills. The set order, meanwhile, helps with the task of memorising – though in real life, in debate as much as in combat, one would improvise.

It is important to remember that in the event of a real debate you will need to build up the strength of your position by degrees. In other words never use your best argument at the beginning. It may be unnecessary to do so, and also way above the head of your opponent. This is why the form appears twice, over these two chapters, because we are going to examine each critique on two different levels. Firstly, we will be looking at sparring, or argument conducted at a fairly lightweight, conversational pace. Then, later on, we take each encounter on to considerably higher ground, real combat, where your opponent is likely to be tenacious or using debate of a fairly heavyweight intellectual class, either in conversation or – perhaps – as part of an ongoing correspondence.

	Critique	Sparring Chapter 7, page	Combat Chapter 8, page
1	Popular Astrology	83	90
2	Twins	83	92
3	Earth-centred	84	96
4	Nations and Peoples	84	100
5	Zodiac	84	107
6	New Planets	85	113
7	Conception	85	116
8	Fatalism	85	121
9	Forced Births	86	125
10	Paganism	87	128
11	Influence	87	136
12	Relevance	88	149

The table above shows the separate components of our 'form' – the twelve types of critique, together with the page numbers where each appears and where you can locate firstly the more lightweight sparring approach, and then the more evolved combat procedure for dealing with each one. Just about any kind of attack will fall into one of these categories but as the discussion develops you may need to draw upon more than one to maintain your position and, ultimately, to neutralise your opponent.

Sparring

The twelve types of critique now follow in the order of the form as shown in the table above – simple but effective defensive responses for each one.

Remember, with sparring, to keep your approach and technique simple, your voice firm and yet sympathetic. There is nothing to be gained here in overcoming your opponent at this stage. This is the true essence of sparring, which allows both parties to learn from the experience.

Critique 1: Popular Astrology

'Astrology can't work. There are only twelve star signs and yet millions of people! You can't tell me that a twelfth of the entire population all have the same horoscope.'

Sparring: 'You're talking about pop astrology, the stuff you read in newspapers or see on TV. They do the best they can, but it's not real astrology: it's journalism, show business. A professional astrologer, on the other hand, will want to know the exact time and place you were born, as well as your birth date, so he or she can calculate what is called a birth chart, a detailed map of the sky that applies to you alone. This makes each individual unique, not just one of millions. Only then can any serious attempt at making predictions be possible.

'Naturally, pop astrology and this rather unfortunate facet of journalism is a constant source of embarrassment to genuine astrologers. At times, some have tried to change their image, calling themselves cosmobiologists or astral scientists. But most astrologers find these terms rather pretentious and that they only serve to confuse the public.'

Critique 2: Twins

'If the birth time is so important for astrology, what about twins? Some twins are born within minutes of each other, but lead different lives. One twin might even die young while the other lives on to a ripe old age. This shows astrology can't work.'

Sparring: 'Even a few minutes can make a lot of difference to a birth chart. That's why all reputable astrologers insist on working with as accurate a birth time as possible. Twins may not always share the same characteristics, of course, but their lives do generally develop at a similar pace. The differences when they occur are subtle ones, which is exactly what astrology would expect. Even in your example, where one twin dies while the other lives, clearly the same event, namely death, has entered both lives at the same time. One twin dies, while the other is touched radically by the sorrow and tragedy of the death of the other. Surely this is an argument for, rather than against, astrology?'

Critique 3: Earth-centred

'Doesn't astrology and all that stuff still put the Earth at the centre of the universe? It's centuries behind the times.'

Sparring: 'Not at all. Astrologers, like most educated people, realise that the Earth is a planet that revolves around the Sun. It's simply more convenient to chart astronomical positions as they appear from the Earth because, after all, it's right here on the Earth that we all have to live. Astrology is concerned with people. And people live on the Earth.'

Critique 4: Nations, Economies and Peoples

'What about when there is a catastrophe involving hundreds of people? Or wars? Would all the people who died in the Hiroshima bomb or on 9/11 have all had the same fate written in their stars?'

Sparring: 'There are, of course, astrological charts for nations as well as for individual people. There are charts for governments, great historical events, and so on. In fact, the study of these is one of the oldest forms of astrology, called Mundane Astrology – taken from the Latin word for 'world'. Naturally, any individual life takes place within this greater framework.'

Critique 5: Zodiac

'Isn't the zodiac just an optical illusion? The stars in each sign are all different distances from us, aren't they, and not connected in any way? It isn't real.'

Sparring: 'Well, yes, the zodiac is composed of stars at different distances, just as a landscape painting is made up of separate elements at different distances, the trees and hills and so on. The picture is a reality in its own right, of course; and so is the zodiac.

'The modern astrologer's zodiac is something different again, though. You are probably confusing this with the actual constellations, the old imaginary pictures in the sky. The modern zodiac has more to do with the seasons and the relationship of the Earth in its orbit about the Sun than with actual groups of stars. In one form or another this kind of zodiac – called the tropical zodiac – has been around for a long time. The Egyptians had it; the Greeks had it. Hundreds of generations have come and gone; people like you and me have lived and died but the zodiac is still there – if that's not real, what is?'

Critique 6: New Planets

'Science has come up with all these new planets, though, hasn't it? Pluto and Uranus and so on. It changes the whole system. Astrologers can't ignore this sort of thing, can they?'

Sparring: 'No, nor would they wish to. Astrologers do in fact welcome the discovery of planets such as Uranus, Neptune and Pluto. They help enormously in the business of character analysis and prediction. Incidentally, astrologers in England had already anticipated the existence of Pluto some twenty years before its actual discovery by the astronomers in 1930.'[1]

Critique 7: Conception

'Astrologers state that they rely on birth times for their work. But surely it's the moment of conception, when all our genetic characteristics come together, which marks the real beginning of the individual existence.'

Sparring: 'Actually the old astrologers thought about this a lot, too. They would set up conception charts as well as birth charts. Precise formulae existed for calculating these, but naturally no one could ever confirm whether they were correct. The relevance of birth charts, on the other hand, has been confirmed through centuries of continued use. In any case, even the geneticists admit that there is a lot more goes into the making of a human being than just inherited characteristics. Astrology deals with the whole, the emerging individual at the time of birth.'

Critique 8: Fatalism

'I don't believe in fate. I'm my own man. I'm not subservient to anything or anyone. And I don't need any astrologer to tell me how to live, or what to do.'

Sparring: 'Telling someone how to live his or her life is the last thing any reputable astrologer would want to do. But it's worth bearing in mind that even the best of us are subservient to our

RS.P.

passions and ambitions at times, which are not always under our conscious control. Astrology can shed some light on these, while recognising all the time that each person is a totally free and independent being, capable of making his or her own decisions.'

Critique 9: Forced Births

'These days, there's hardly any such thing as a natural birth. Babies are induced artificially or even created in test tubes! Doesn't this somehow throw astrology out?'

Sparring: 'Not in the least. A birth time is a birth time, no matter what circumstances surround it. Everyone is born at the right time, regardless of what procedures may take place in hospitals. On balance, however, astrologers do disapprove of induced births, since there is some statistical evidence to suggest that it destroys a certain natural affinity between parent and child.'[2]

Critique 10: Paganism

'Astrology is a wicked, pagan superstition. As a Christian, one naturally believes that God has endowed mankind with free will. To consult the planets about the future is a primitive, heathen practice.'

Sparring: 'On a popular level, it may seem so. However, real astrology, as practised by the professional, has always recognised the dominance of individual free will. Apart from that, there are many astrologers who are also practising Christians. Even those who are not have absolutely no desire to encourage worship of pagan gods, Jupiter, Saturn, and so on. Rather, they use these bodies to represent psychological or spiritual realities. The blend of Christianity and astrology has a long history, as well. Many of the founding fathers of the Church, for example, were sympathetic to astrology, recognising its importance in both the Jewish and Neo-Platonic traditions from which Christianity derived so much of its inspiration.'

Critique 11: Influence

'How can the planets have any effect on us? I've never felt anything. You can't tell me that a few lumps of rock and gas millions of miles away can exert any kind of influence.'

Sparring: 'Well, they do. Influences from such distances are being recorded all the time. Astronomical phenomena affect everything from the quality of radio transmissions to the degree of haemorrhages during surgical operations.

'Anyway, astrologers can get along quite comfortably without the need for influences. They work on what is called synchronicity. For example, farmers will tell you that certain migrating birds will invariably leave early before a hard winter, long before any change in the weather that might suggest what is to come. The birds' migration doesn't influence the cold winter any more than the movements of the planets need to influence you and me. They happen together, that's all, and if we use our experience we can draw some useful conclusions about the future.'

Critique 12: Relevance

'Astrology is just old hat, isn't it? It's like religion; people are too smart these days to be taken in by magic and superstition.'

Sparring: 'Perhaps it's not so important in your life, or amongst the people you know, but take my word for it, astrology is still as widespread and popular today as ever. Astrology has nothing to do with magic either, and has plenty of modern practical uses, everything from career planning to stock market speculation. Yes, it does have a spiritual dimension. Most of the really worthwhile things in life do. This does no harm, though, and can do a lot of good.'

So much for sparring, in which our replies have been kept deliberately brief and rather superficial. In the next chapter, however, it is assumed that your adversaries will be equipped with a moderate knowledge of astronomy and general science. Arming yourself in turn with these really not too daunting technicalities can no longer be avoided, since the subject must be thoroughly understood. This level of understanding needs to be maintained in an up-to-date fashion, moreover, if you are to take on any of the really heavyweight challenges that we are going to meet with next. This book will help, of course, but if you are not yet confident of this level of understanding, then your local library or the internet will be able to supply you with a good general background on the kind of topics covered – astronomy, biology, the arts, comparative religion, and so on – all areas touched on by astrology to some extent. Often, even the most esteemed of professional astrologers are found sorely lacking in this kind of knowledge, and so it's advisable to keep up to speed from time to time on the technical side of the subject, otherwise your arguments will be flawed and your entire stance vulnerable to anyone already well versed in these fields.

CHAPTER 8

Combat

This is the second, more advanced version of the form. Each critique is treated at considerable length now, and obviously you are not intended to memorise every word, nor would this be of much use anyway. As previously mentioned, the separate elements have to be employed creatively and matched to the demands of the moment. Also the full extent of each reply is never likely to be needed in the general conversational situation. What is presented here is somewhat of an ideal scenario: two people addressing each other courteously in a quiet room with lots and lots of time to spare. Does this ever happen? It is possible, however, that you might wish to employ a larger amount of the material in correspondence, in which case you will be able to enhance it and amend it with whatever latest research is at hand. But note ... the basic framework of each section has been carefully structured for maximum effect, and this plan of attack should still be of use even when you wish to make extensive changes and additions of your own.

You can, of course, expect interruptions that may break your concentration and tempt you to interrupt back. Ultimately this can only result in an argument or slanging match and must be avoided by making it clear that you have no wish to discuss the subject in anything other than a calm and sensible manner. No one will ever blame you for wanting to treat the debate seriously, certainly not at this level, but any hint of impatience or hysteria can cast a shadow of doubt over even the finest of speakers. At all times do not lose sight of the basic principles outlined in previous chapters. Stance and attitude remain as important during real combat as they are during the casual opening of the encounter. Relaxation should also not be lost. This is vital. Yield when necessary; be firm when you need to.

So, let us recommence the form: each critique appears in the same order as in the previous chapter on sparring, and as shown in the table on page 82.

Critique 1: Popular Astrology

'Although I appreciate the distinction between pop astrology and the professional work which treats each person individually, the fact that the same language and terminology is shared by both types of astrology, suggests that they must also share the same principles. If newspaper astrology is nonsense, how can the other version practised by the esteemed professional be anything other than a more refined kind of nonsense?'

Note: Here it is obviously going to be necessary to explain some of the basic principles of real astrology. There is a lot to tell, of course, but don't become too involved or worry if you leave things out. Your explanation should be styled merely to demonstrate the depth and complexity of the subject. Unless you and your opponent have a fair smattering of astronomical knowledge, such a task would be futile in any case. Keeping this in mind, proceed along the following lines:

Combat: 'Genuine astrology is not a refinement of pop astrology, as some people seem to think. Pop or newspaper astrology is a wholly modern, and entirely degenerate offshoot of the mainstream profession. Popular astrology simply draws on one small working principle from the vast range of traditional astrological practice, namely the Sun signs of its readers, in order to make a few general sweeping pronouncements. These are, in any case, couched in such nebulous terms as to be virtually meaningless. Furthermore, when you consider that astrology can trace its origins back thousands of years, and that the popular offshoot appeared only as recently as the 1930s, it is obvious which has the greater pedigree.

'To explain why popular astrology is such a debasement of the real thing, requires a little technical understanding of the subject. To begin with, simply knowing the birthday of someone is of no use whatsoever to any serious astrologer. Rather, precise and complete data are needed, including year, time and place of birth, in order to plot the positions of the Sun, Moon and planets on to a detailed map called a birth, or natal, chart. This process will also reveal many additional factors such as the ascending and culminating degrees of the ecliptic for that locality, and the actual house system of the chart derived from these points.

'Any number of these features can be activated by current, day-to-day movements in the heavens called transits. Not only this, but movements shortly before and shortly after birth are also taken into account in a complex business of forecasting called progressions. So, to produce a satisfactory forecast for any one year, for example, a genuine professional astrologer specialising in this field will need to spend several hours, if not a whole day or two, firstly on calculating and studying the natal chart, and then later looking at how this will relate to astonomical movements, transits and progressions, pertaining to that year. At the same time the astrologer will carefully balance all this data with knowledge of the client's background, environment, and state of health, to come to some realistic conclusions about the future.

'Newspaper forecasting, on the other hand, is usually run off in a matter of a few minutes, furnishing the entire population with so-called predictions in the space of just one or two brief columns. Obviously in this process something has to go. In fact almost everything goes, except for that one piece of data: the approximate location of the Sun on the birthdays of the readers. This is only possible because the Sun returns to roughly the same position on any given day each and every year. So, for example, if you are born anywhere between the 23 August and 22 September the pop astrologer knows, regardless of your age, that your Sun was somewhere within the sign of Virgo at birth. He can then look at approximate daily movements of Moon and Sun and relate these to the general thirty-degree area of the zodiac that corresponds to Virgo. If extraordinarily conscientious, our Sun-sign astrologer might also check on the daily movements of the planet Mercury, which traditionally rules the sign of Virgo and corresponds closely to it, to ascertain whether this body has any aspects – angular relationships – to any other planets that might be significant.

'These form the basis of any so-called predictions. All the other factors normally pertaining to individual birth charts, which vary not only from year to year but from day to day, hour to hour and minute to minute, are totally ignored.

'So, yes, there is just that little bit of common language between pop astrology and the real thing. But to criticise real astrology because of the vagaries of journalism and TV entertainment is rather like judging the entire medical profession on the efficacy of grandma's medicine cupboard.'

Note: At this point you should also make it clear that genuine, quality astrology does not concern itself exclusively with prediction. Natal astrology – that is, interpretation of the birth chart in terms of character and self-expression – often comprises the bulk of the modern astrologer's work. You can even stress that some consultants occupy themselves exclusively with character analysis and counselling, and refuse to have anything to do with forecasting. They advocate that character itself is destiny, and that when a strong individual will is involved, hard-and-fast predictions are meaningless, anyway.

If you really want to press home your attack, mention the branches of horary astrology, mundane and electional astrology and also financial astrology. You can confidently refer your opponent to any one of the many excellent introductory books that are mentioned in the reading list at the end of this book or on our website.

Critique 2: Twins

'Everyone knows that twins, especially identical twins born within a few minutes of each other, share many characteristics. These, however, are genetic in origin. If astrology were true, all babies, regardless of parentage, born in the same hospital within a few minutes of each other would be almost identical. This is clearly not so.'

Combat: 'Sorry to disappoint you, but it is so – or at least sometimes. We call such babies, born at the same time in roughly the same place, 'time twins'. And there have been numerous documented cases throughout the world, and throughout history, of such people and the remarkable similarities in their lives. Not only do time twins often look alike, but sometimes, unknown to each other, lead lives of remarkable similarity. Examples exist of time twins who marry in the same year, have the same number of children, and even experience accidents and injury at similar times. Often the family backgrounds of these children are the same, too, the number of brothers and sisters, the father's occupation and so on.[1]

'Actually, time twins probably lead lives of such similarity precisely because they are not aware of each other. Real twins who live and grow together naturally strive to diverge at times. After all, no one, not even the most devoted of identical twins, wants to be a carbon copy of somebody else. That's why the most startling stories of time twins are of the ones who know nothing of each other's existence, until some quirk of fate brings them together. Then, the media catch hold of the story and it makes the headlines for a while. Probably most of us who were born in a big city have a time twin or two somewhere, though of course we rarely meet them – and until recently, moreover, there had been little consistent research into the subject.[2]

'Of the numerous, famous and quite stunning examples of time twins that have been recorded, one of the most entertaining is the oft-quoted, though admittedly largely unverified story of King George III of England and Samuel Hemming. Hemming was a commoner in eighteenth-century England, but shared the same time and date of birth as the king. Hemming took over his father's business as ironmonger on the same day George succeeded to the throne. Both Hemming and George were married on the same day, and ultimately each had the same number of children of the same sex. Accidents and illness occurred on similar dates, and they both died on the same day from similar causes.

'Among the more recent documented examples, is the early motion picture industry's search for a double to Rudolph Valentino after his death. One of the most convincing candidates turned out to have been born in the same area and on the same day as Valentino.[3]

'Another report from the last century concerns two American girls who met at the age of six, when their families moved next door to each other. Although unrelated, they looked and behaved like identical twins, and teachers and parents alike had difficulty distinguishing between the two. The girls each had the same number of brothers and sisters; in fact the two families shared almost identical physical likenesses, not only between the girls and the two sets of parents, but also between the brothers and sisters. Both fathers worked in the same place at similar jobs. Later research revealed that the two girls had been born within five minutes of each other at the same nursing home.[4]

'In another example, an astrologer tells of how he once encountered his "double", a man who had the same appearance, same scars, same dental condition, everything. He discovered that the double had lived a life that closely resembled his own in terms of experiences and dates of events; whereas one was an astrologer with antiques as a hobby, the other was an antique fancier with astrology as a hobby. They were time twins.[5]

'There is clearly a lot of anecdotal evidence at large here. But something unusual is obviously at work, too. Astrologers have a way of debating this phenomena and making sense of it – that's all.'

Note: Having said this, it is only fair to point out that not every case of identical births produces time twins with matching characters and life stories. Far from it! Your opponent may well suspect as much and interrupt you at some stage with something like:

Interruption: 'Surely you don't mean to say that every child born at the same time and place as another will have identical life stories?'

Counter-attack: 'No. And, indeed, really striking cases of time twins tend to be the exception rather than the rule – and until recently there has been little consistent research into this subject so that we might compare them to check for similarities. The pioneering work of John Addey in the late sixties was followed by that of Roberts and Greengrass in 1994 who enlisted help from the media to gather data on 128 people born just over an hour apart.[6] Their conclusions were impressive, and has lifted the study of time twins beyond the purely anecdotal which has been the cause of so much criticism in the past. One of the most newsworthy pairings that they discovered was two time twins with similarities of interest and occupation – the one twin being a clarinet player, the other a bassoon player!

'You are right in being sceptical, however. The issue of time twins has been a cause for much debate in recent times between astrologers and their detractors – the latter sensing a subject over which they can exert some critical muscle by enlisting statistical research. For example, there are undoubtedly cases of recorded time twins in which the subjects were found to have led dramatically different lives and developed highly disparate personalities.[7] Moreover, it must be said that statistical data of this kind can be interpreted differently and different studies can even be slanted in such a way as to make time twins look like a complete fiction.[8] For example, what exactly constitutes a valid time frame for gathering data on time twins? Should they be born within minutes of each other, or is it OK to study pairs born several hours apart? Clearly, the wider the time frame for gathering data, the more likely the phenomenon is to break down.

'Astrologers aren't disturbed by any of this, of course, since even in those cases where the characters of closely born time twins diverge, it simply demonstrates the environmental factor, genetic inheritance and the use of self-determination in the lives of those individuals concerned, something any professional astrologer worth their salt would welcome and encourage. For example, one time twin may be blessed with genes that make a particular course of action more likely – aggression, for example, leading to more self-assertion. The other time twin may possess a milder genetic heritage and therefore not make the same radical choices in life or encounter the same opportunities. They may have a genetic predisposition to a particular illness, heart disease, diabetes and so on, which will shape one of the time twin's life profoundly compared to the other who may have been blessed with perfect health. Some environmental differences can also be quite overwhelming: the upbringing or material wealth of the parents, the type of schooling, and so on. After all, we are all of us much more than the mere slavish fulfilment of our birth charts or our genes, and all these additional factors can produce changes that can appear to make the time twins' lives dramatically different. All this is to be expected in the real world with all its diversity and range of opportunities and is something that will always make the gathering of evidence for time twins quite challenging.

'Also we may well be missing the fact here that there could be shared characteristics between time twins that have been internalised instead of being visibly obvious. Perhaps there is a common identity of purpose between the twins, which may not be immediately evident to the observer in search of external traits – a common ambition, for instance, or a shared phobia. Astrology will always manifest in different ways. Clearly, with time twins, those truly remarkable instances where similarities are revealed in a physical sense are in no way diminished by those cases in which they are not. Ultimately, too, the cases of really closely matching time twins are so extraordinary that they cannot simply be brushed aside.'

Critique 3: Earth-centred

'The arrival of the Copernican theory in the sixteenth century totally destroyed the old medieval view of a geocentric universe. From this time on, educated men and women no longer bowed to the old religious and scholastic dogma of the Middle Ages. The mistaken view that the Earth and all of humankind were at the centre of creation became redundant, and the entire metaphysical and theological structure of antiquity collapsed, taking along with it the old superstitions like astrology and magic.

'We now know that the Earth is simply a planet, among many planets, orbiting the Sun – itself a star, a mere speck within the galaxy of stars that is itself a mere point of light in the vastness of space. Astrology, in the face of such knowledge, is meaningless.'

Combat: 'Your critique is fairly representative of popular academic opinion, but it also contains a number of common inaccuracies. Firstly, the Copernican hypothesis was not the finished heliocentric theory as we know it today, nor was it at the time anything new. The earliest known statement against the Earth-centred view appears as far back as the Pythagoreans in the fifth century BC. Philolaus, Pythagoras's pupil, certainly considered the idea that the Earth, Sun and all the planets revolved about a central fire. It is quite likely that Pythagoras himself also believed this and that in one version of the theory the central fire was meant to be the Sun itself.[9]

'Much, if not the bulk of the teachings of Pythagoras came directly from the Egyptian and Babylonian scholars with whom, it is thought, he studied during his youth. So the idea that the astronomers of antiquity only ever regarded the Earth as immobile and at the centre is almost certainly wrong. Remember, the Egyptian and Persian sciences were esoteric, never committed to writing. We have no way of knowing for sure if they had a heliocentric view of the cosmos, but in the light of Pythagoras and his ideas it is certainly possible. And if so, the hypothesis could have an even greater antiquity than the Pythagoreans themselves!

'The earliest documented and purely heliocentric theory we know of, however, was that of Aristarchus in the third century BC. Although, like so many other precious volumes of the classical world, Aristarchus's original work has not survived, the theory itself was freely available to Roman scholars in the early centuries of our era, and the concept must certainly have lingered on in the minds of the Arab and European scientists of the Middle Ages, becoming ultimately the inspiration behind the new heliocentric system of the Renaissance to which you refer.

'The reason for the survival and almost universal preference for the geocentric system among medieval scholars was partly because it was the one preferred by Claudius Ptolemy, who flourished around the second century and is perhaps still the best-known of the Greek cosmographers. Of equal importance, however, was that the Earth-centred view of the universe was also the only one that could produce reliable ephemeredes, or tables of future planetary positions. Therefore, the heliocentric option remained largely of academic interest only and became more and more neglected as time went on. It was not entirely forgotten, however, and the German astrologer and cardinal Nicolaus of Cusa, who flourished a century before Copernicus, favoured and taught the heliocentric theory to his own followers.

'There were, however, also aesthetic and theological grounds for taking the Earth as the centre, deeply profound ones, inspired by the philosophies of the Neo-Platonists and, therefore, of Pythagoras and the ancient world itself. This consisted of a mystical relationship between mankind and the cosmos, in which enlightenment and wisdom were gained through prayer, meditation or magical ritual. It was the ascent of the spirit or soul, upwards from the earthly elements, through each of the planetary spheres to the *primum mobile* and the realm of the Unmoved Mover. Much of this was metaphoric, and was recognised and accepted as such by the Church. It was seen as one of the many possible experiences of union with God in Christian Neo-Platonism: unity of the individual with the Infinite, similar to that found in other cultures the world over – in the art of Shamanism, for example, or in the search for Samadhi achieved through the practice of yoga.

'But, as already mentioned, the most persuasive force in favour of the geocentric option remained that of a simple, irrefutable practicality. Even with the increasingly sophisticated observations of the Middle Ages, the geocentric-based equations still managed to account adequately for planetary motion, including retro-gradation, which is when the planets appear to backtrack across the sky for certain periods. The mathematicians had always managed to make adjustments for the phenomenon through the use of what are called epicycles. An epicycle is the circular motion of, say, a planet about a central point that is itself in orbit around another body, say the Earth: a complex system of wheels within wheels, in other words. By the thirteenth century there were no less than around sixty of these hypothetical epicycles used in calculating ephemeredes. Obviously there was constant experimentation with alternative systems and models, and it is quite reasonable to suppose that heliocentricity was among them, especially in the light of the links between classical Greece and the Arab world where most of the technical advances were being made up until the time of the Renaissance. Epicycles, and the Earth-centred models, however, still seemed to work the best, and were therefore retained.

'For all its practicality and usefulness, however, its absurd complexity must have been apparent to all educated men. It would have naturally raised suspicions in the minds of many. The learned thirteenth-century King of Leon and Castille, Alphonso X, responsible for the most accurate ephemeredes of the Middle Ages, is reported to have quipped that had he been around at the time of the creation, he could have handed out some useful advice – perhaps, we must assume, concerning a less complex layout for the solar system. Yet he knew as well as anyone that to abandon the geocentric tradition at that stage would have been impractical and unnecessary.

'With the European Renaissance came the rediscovery of classical ideas and theories, and, as I have mentioned, men such as Nicolaus of Cusa considered a Sun-centred system very early on. However, it is the later name of Copernicus that is most often associated with the new outlook. Himself an astrologer and an enthusiast of Pythagorean teaching, Copernicus published his own version of a heliocentric model for the solar system in 1543. Yet this was at the time hardly the startling, anti-establishment tract that historians have subsequently urged us to believe. Its contents even had papal approval! – a far cry from the tribulations suffered by the more radical Galileo less than a century later. Nor were astrologers at all piqued by the new theory. It was certainly never considered a threat. For one thing, it furnished them with far more accurate tables of planetary motion. Moreover, the Copernican theory still required epicycles to account for certain irregularities, and the real breakthrough came only much later, in the seventeenth century with the work of Johannes Kepler.

'Kepler abandoned the idea of circular orbits for the planets and plumped for ellipses instead. At a stroke, the vastly complex epicycle systems were demolished, and a purely heliocentric model, which actually *worked,* was finally reinstated. Again, the important thing about this development was that it produced more reliable ephemeredes upon which astronomers and astrologers alike could base their work, while at the same time opening the way for a total rebirth of Pythagorean metaphysics and astronomical mysticism.

Kepler himself was at the forefront of this kind of research. For Kepler, a highly religious man as well as an astrologer and a Pythagorean scholar, the central fire of the Sun now became synonymous with God the Father. Kepler was also able to discover remarkably close correlations between the distance-ratios of the planetary orbits and the five basic solids of Platonic philosophy, and he speculated on musical theories, awarding to each planet a range of notes based on the eccentricity of its orbit about the Sun, an echo of Pythagoras's music of the spheres.

'In other words, none of these highly interesting developments in astronomical theory which took us closer and closer to heliocentricity over the years, ever made the slightest difference to those practising astrology – apart, that is, from the welcome increase in accuracy that the new system brought with it. The partial demise of astrology and magic that you mentioned took place only gradually and then not to any significant degree until a century or so later, around the time of Newton. Reasons for this decline were many and complex, and owed as much to the rise of commercial maritime power in the seventeenth century, which used the stars for navigation and trade, and therefore for making money, as it did to the theories of Copernicus over a century earlier.

'Happily, in our own times, modern relativity theory provides us with a legitimate choice in the matter. Here, space, time, and motion are all seen as interchangeable. It is just as valid to consider the Sun revolving around the Earth, as it is the other way around. The more basic mathematical concept of reflective symmetry had also always allowed for this reversal if need be, something that was well known in Copernicus's time, incidentally, and even to a certain extent in the era of Ptolemy.

'Astrology has survived all these fluctuating ideas and notions. It continues to measure angular relationships of planets to the Earth and still draws the Earth at the centre of its charts. This is because astrology remains a subject for humankind, for people. We do, after all, live on the Earth. In other words each of us is at the centre of his or her own cosmos.

'Very well – as a scientist or astronomer – you can tell me that all this is senseless and that we actually live on a speck of dust orbiting around a tiny star lost in the billions of stars that make up our galaxy, which is itself an insignificant grain in the vastness of space. You can tell me that one of the nearest galaxies stands at a distance of more than two million light years, and that a voice from such a place would be just that number of years old and presumably very, very dead by the time it reached us. You can even imply that all the achievements of humanity are nothing more than the blind helpless grovellings of primitive animals on a lump of decaying rock and gas lost in the cold eternity of space and time. But then tell me just one more thing – where's the sense in that?

'At least astrology deals with life as we know it, with our environment and our feelings, with our loves and the warm comfort of our common humanity. Copernicus considering that the Earth might, after all, go around the Sun doesn't suddenly destroy all that, and your suggestion that his work might have somehow rendered astrology meaningless is really untenable.

'Ultimately, I suppose, it all depends on your point of view, whether you are at the centre of understanding or merely looking in from the periphery.'

Critique 4: Nations, Economies and Peoples

'While one can readily appreciate that an individual life takes place within the larger framework of the State, and that individual birth charts are subservient to national ones, why is there such a shortage of accurate predictions in political or national affairs? When the hijacked planes flew into the twin towers of the World

Trade Center in New York in September 2001, it was not only a day on which much of our modern world changed for ever, but also a day when the final nail was driven into the astrological coffin. Surely something so devastating, so threatening to our economies, our social establishment, institutions and laws should have been discernible in the stars? If your mundane astrology is a workable reality, how is it that astrologers in this field have no real documented successes? These would, surely, make the headlines, and prove astrology to all.'

Combat: 'There are, in fact, many well-documented predictions in the field of mundane astrology that have been fulfilled, both in the past and in recent times. For example, the nuclear catastrophe at Chernobyl in 1986, and also the English Channel ferry disaster of 1987.[10] The first Gulf War in 1990. And the recent wars in Afghanistan and Iraq and, indeed, the economic and global crises that occurred on and immediately following 9/11, were also all successfully predicted.[11]

'I should like to tell you about some of these predictions in just a moment, but first I'd like to get all this into some kind of perspective. It is certainly true to say that astrologers working in this field tend to face some of the most difficult challenges of all in astrology, and they have not always had an easy time of it. In the past many predictions were kept in private hands due to their sensitivity and political importance. Many were also suppressed by governments who often viewed pronouncements on the state of the nation as potentially bad propaganda. This was as true in twentieth-century Germany under the Third Reich as it was in antiquity under the emperors of Rome.

'Setting aside anecdotal evidence for a moment, and looking at those predictions that have survived from history, we find that the most famous to come down to us are, of course, those of Nostradamus, the sixteenth-century mystic and astrologer. Included in his rather cryptic works are allusions to most of the great conflicts and political figures of his era, and much of Nostradamus's work is still thought to bear directly on events in our own times.[12]

'In his day, Nostradamus was consulted by many powerful and influential persons such as Henry II of France and Catherine de Medici, and it is this commissioned use of mundane astrology that is still very much in evidence today. Many of the most

101

powerful and influential men and women in the world, particularly in the American continent, Japan and the Middle East, take on board the counselling of astrologers as part of their overall world view. It provides them with a totally independent, alternative strategy, as distinct from orthodox informed analysis, and thus enables them to stay one step ahead of most developments. Much of this work is, by its nature, confidential and unpublished – but, as recent "revelations" seem to indicate, astrology of this kind has extended right up to the White House and the Kremlin.

'It's not all hush-hush, though. In our own times there has been considerable open research into the subject of political and economic astrology, including published data, periodicals, and so on. These are readily available and deal capably, in so far as is possible for such a complex subject, with trends and developments in political and economic affairs. If you are looking for spectacular predictions of wars, assassinations and tragedies, however, you may be disappointed. Modern astrologers do not deal in crystal gazing, and although certain significators are almost always present in the charts of sudden and dramatic world events, the converse is by no means always true. The charts of nations often produce quite violent features from time to time that correlate to nothing at all in real terms.

'Although essentially superior in their scope to individual birth charts, national charts lend themselves far less readily to the difficult business of prediction. This is because whereas each human individual has only one possible chart: the one recorded for his or her birth time, nations, on the other hand, often have several valid charts. Britain, for example, has at least three, including the chart for the coronation of William the Conqueror in 1066, and that for the birth of the United Kingdom in 1801. Thankfully, in these cases the birth times were well documented. In most instances, however, it is far from easy to determine exactly when a nation begins and what events actually constitute that beginning. Is it the signing of a document, or the moment of surrender on a battlefield? Is it the storming of a palace or parliament, or the speech of a great prophet or leader? The answer can be yes to any one of these, and more. Records of such moments are often incomplete, or tend to present several alternatives, as in the case of the USA Declaration of Independence, which has several possible birth times, which are still to this day hotly disputed by astrologers.

'Moreover, the birth charts for the leaders of each nation are often paramount in this respect and far outweigh the considerations of the national map. National events often show up clearly in the charts of a Royal Family, for example, or of the Prime Minister, or President, while charts cast for the taking of office, inaugurations, or the official results of an election, can also prove significant depending on how closely these relate to the welfare of the nation in question. Of course, as critics correctly point out, in a sense the astrologer working in the mundane field is able to hedge his bets considerably because of this wide range of possible sources. There will always be a chart somewhere that will relate to a real event when looking retrospectively. The trick, of course, is in finding the right one and making a forecast before the event occurs.

'It might also be fair to say that certain real-time planetary configurations, called transits, could be so potent in their own right at certain localities as totally to override individual national considerations and individual charts, be it of people or of nations. Don't forget, the words 'catastrophe' and 'disaster' each have their root in the Latin *astra* meaning star, and observations of such configurations were actually the backbone of political and economic astrology in antiquity.

'So, you see, mundane astrology is a complex business: sadly, perhaps the most nebulous and ill-defined part of the whole subject. That is why it is totally unrealistic to expect astrologers to measure up to some kind of biblical standard of prophesy in this or indeed in any other field. Though, having said this, if you care to investigate current work, particularly that of astrological correlations to cycles in the world economy, I think you may well be favourably impressed by the accuracy of some of the more conservative and sober predictions. Notable examples in recent times are those of Daniel Pallant, an investment analyst specialising in astrology, who occasionally writes for the financial press in the UK. His forecast of January 1987, for example, of an FTSE Index level of 2216 by 11 May from its then level of 1675 was indeed fulfilled, in fact just a few days later than predicted, on 19 May. Perhaps only those familiar with the capriciousness of world stock markets will appreciate just how exceptionally accurate this prediction was.

'The American market, as might be expected, also has its astrological pundits and, arguably one of the best, Arch Crawford, who is regularly ranked among the top market-timers on Wall Street. Such a ranking, based on concrete demonstrable performance, is no mean feat when you recall that the competition here would be drawn from among all the other many top technical and fundamental analysts that ply their trade on Wall Street. In 2002, according to *Hulbert Financial Digest,* Crawford made a 46.7 per cent return on his timing calls.

'Crawford is also quite unusual in not being averse to sticking his neck out occasionally and putting his views to the test. Many of his predictions have been captured in major media outlets such as *The Wall Street Journal, Barron's, Forbes, Business Week, New York Post, Chicago Tribune, Miami Herald, Institutional Investor* and *CNBC.* Many of these predictions, moreover, illustrate the working reality of mundane and financial astrology very well, and the realistic extent to which we can expect events to be spelled out in absolute terms.

'As I hope I have made clear already, work of this kind does not avail itself of a crystal ball at any stage but simply works on the basis of probabilities. For instance, although the start of the first Gulf War was predicted by Crawford, it was not possible, like many predictions of this kind, to pinpoint the very place where it would happen. Crawford could only say that something big was going to happen somewhere in the world that would effect the stock market, and that this would occur between 2 August and 7 August that year – stating, too, that the involvement of Mars and Pluto indicated an attempt at coercion, the use of force, and a powerful explosion. Venus opposing Saturn, meanwhile, suggested heartlessness and cruelty.[13] On 2 August precisely, Iraq astonished the world by suddenly invading its neighbour Kuwait.

'Going further back, the great stock market crash of 1987 was also foreseen by Crawford[14] – while the most accurate timing of this particularly devastating event was arguably that of the German-Swiss astro-economist Wolfgang Angermeyer.[15]

'You mentioned the dreadful events of 9/11 – and indeed, what happened on that fateful day does illustrate very clearly the difficulties just outlined. Throughout that year there were a number of destructive and dangerous aspects featuring slow-moving planets that could have been triggered at just about any time by a real event. But it is not always feasible under such conditions to isolate a particularly day or even week when things might actually come to pass, let alone a location. So you are correct, no one at any stage ever came up with a miraculous prediction along the lines that on 11 September 2001 jet planes would be flown into the World Trade Center and the Pentagon with the loss of 3000 lives.

'However, you may be surprised to learn that a major international crisis for that moment was predicted by Wall Street's Crawford, along with the ensuing wars in Afghanistan and the melt-down in the world equity markets that followed. In addition to his clear and unambiguous prediction from May of 2000 of a 'bloody bear market' in six to eighteen months, he also stated in his September 2001 newsletter how we were faced with the darkening of the light. Planetary movements on 8 September would be leading as to war; that the ninth would be another turning point and that financial markets could be occulted (hidden) on 10 to 12 September.[16] Those who follow the stock markets closely will recall that the New York Stock Exchange and the Nasdaq were both shut down on 11 September and for several days immediately afterwards – occulted indeed, and a state of affairs unprecedented in the history of Wall Street. Shortly after the re-opening of the stock market on the following Monday, an estimated $1.38 trillion had been wiped off the value of shares. And as if this wasn't enough, Crawford further stated that for the US it would be warlike action on 2 October. It was indeed.

'Of course, critics of astrology often point out, quite rightly, that although some predictions of this kind do come to fruition, we never hear much about the many others that don't, and which are promptly forgotten. This is true, and illustrates how difficult it is to work in this field without a specific brief from a client or by having the advantage of a specialist subject on which to focus. With around six billion people in over 260 countries, not to mention all the heads of state and industrial leaders, the world stage is simply too vast to be able to look out for every eventuality, which is why specialist astrologers such as Crawford who focus on a more intimate area of knowledge are so visibly successful. The brief here is clear – to watch out for cycles and events that will affect the stock and commodity markets of the world. Get that right and you have a fair chance of highlighting some major social and political events at the same time. And although Crawford would be the first to admit that some of his work also makes use of standard technical analysis as well as astrological cycles, it is clear from the newsletters in question that the predictions concerning September 2001 were largely astrological in content. Ultimately, the proof of the pudding is in the eating, and those who have followed the predictions made by the best astrologers in this field have managed to protect their capital through many of the major turning points and geo-political disasters that have befallen us in these difficult and turbulent times.'

Note: At this point you can perhaps recommend to your opponent the numerous journals and periodicals of organisations such as the Astrological Association of Great Britain, and the equivalent bodies in America, and most European and Commonwealth countries, all generally containing up-to-date articles on this subject. You can find a list of useful addresses on page 215.

Remember, when arguing the case for mundane astrology it is important to communicate the genuine difficulties inherent in this branch of the subject. Moreover, much of what is expected to be the province of mundane astrology, the winning of an election, an abdication, resignation, and so on, is actually often dependent on natal work. Analysis of charts belonging to individuals is essential for this kind of forecasting, and the problem here is that those who are employed on a private basis for this purpose do not, as a rule, publish their findings, while those who are not thus employed must by necessity give only a cursory glance to each element in what is a truly vast field of daily transits, national charts, political institutions and world leaders. It would indeed be a superhuman task to spend even a month of one's life anticipating but a fraction of all the possible permutations of global forecasting. This is why most published work on political affairs tends to consist of 'wise-after-the-event' discussions rather than hard and fast predictions of future events. Moreover, there is no rule that says every event has to have an astrological correlation. Why should it be incumbent on astrology always to have an answer for everything that happens in the world?

Do try to stress these difficulties to your opponent, who may be expecting miracles from those courageous enough to work in the purely political field.

Critique 5: Zodiac

'Owing to what is called precession, or the gradual shifting of the spring equinox, none of the signs of the astrologer's zodiac corresponds any more to the constellation that bears its name. For instance, the astrologer's Sun sign Aries now falls in the neighbouring constellation of Pisces. With every passing 72 years, the astrologers' signs become a further one degree out of phase with the original star patterns. This makes nonsense of the whole subject, as its basis is completely wrong.

'Even if that were not the case, and the zodiac and the constellations had remained in sync', the same since antiquity, it is preposterous to suppose that simply because a few ancient shepherds, or whatever, fancied they could see the shape of, say, a Ram or a Bull in the stars, that this section of the sky should possess the attributes of that creature and subsequently bestow it upon humans who happen to be born during the month when the Sun passes through it. All those stars are at vastly different distances, and not connected in the slightest way. This is the most primitive form of anthropomorphic projection, magical rubbish of the first rank.'

Combat: 'The precession of the equinoxes has been widely known to astronomers and astrologers alike since as early as the third century BC and the observations of Hipparchus. It seems likely that Egyptian, Aztec and, most notably, Chinese astronomers, could have known of it many centuries earlier, and it is possible that some Indian Vedic literature of before 1000 BC alludes to it also.[17]

'Moreover, long before Hipparchus put the notion of precession into writing, the priests and astronomers of the ancient European stone circles will have been aware of it, too, since on the mornings of their festivals they would have recorded how at Sunrise certain stars tended to set in different places from one generation to the next. Don't forget, these great monuments are now known to have been highly sophisticated observatories as well as places of worship. Not only are they of great antiquity, but their working life spanned many centuries. In short, it would be extremely odd if they, or the builders of the Pyramids, had not observed precession and passed this knowledge down through subsequent generations. The knowledge of precession, therefore, might even predate the creation of the zodiac itself.

'The current tropical zodiac, used by astrologers, with its well-known twelve-fold division first appears in the records around the fifth century BC but its basis was originally a four-fold division of the ecliptic circle which emerged out of the natural geographical realities: north, south, east and west and the four quarters of heaven which are enshrined in every occult, religious, architectural and mythological tradition of humankind, from ancient China to Stonehenge, from the Aztec and Greek temples to the Gothic cathedrals of Europe. This is precisely why in each quarter of our tropical zodiac you will find firstly one Cardinal sign, which begins directly on the solstice or equinox, followed by one Fixed sign which marks the middle of the quarter and consequently of the season, and finally, at the close, one Mutable sign that leads up to the next quarter, marking, therefore, a time of change when each season gives way to a new.

'Yes, the conventional astrologer's zodiac does now begin in a different place in the sky compared to the backdrop of stars two thousand years ago. That's perfectly correct, because almost all zodiacs are and always have been fundamentally Sun-based, linked to the geographical co-ordinates, and are only incidentally projected on to the background of stars when necessary. These co-ordinates naturally change with time, taking the seasonal zodiac along with them. This, and the calendar that inevitably arises from it, is something that has always been present, vital in its regularity to all the affairs of humankind and the natural world, particularly agriculture and navigation. Constellations and individual stars have only ever been noted in so far as they provided markers for these all-important activities – as, for example in *The Works and Days,* the agricultural poem and calendar of Hesiod in the eighth century BC.

'Therefore, while acutely aware of the distinction you have mentioned, almost all astrologers from at least the time of Ptolemy in the second century AD have chosen to adhere to the zodiac based on the moving equinoctial points, the tropical zodiac, as it is called, rather than the constellations. There is constant experimentation, however, on the part of astrologers to determine whether the so-called fixed stars have any relevance or not. The astrologers who advocate the use of star groups as a basis for their co-ordinates are called siderealists. There are a few of these in the West, and the sidereal system, or a variation of it, is still in use in Indian astrology.

'The sidereal zodiac has many disadvantages, however, which render it unworkable for most modern astrologers. Firstly – not really too serious but still worth mentioning – that the stars themselves are not truly fixed at all, but have a slow drift of their own in the sky: proper motion, as it is termed. The star Aldebaran in the constellation of Taurus, for example, has shifted over one minute of arc since Roman times, and this is by no means the fastest. Proper motion of as much as ten seconds per year has been detected.

'Secondly, and more significantly, the boundaries of the constellations themselves are irregular and do not permit the exact harmonic division of the circle that constitutes the modern zodiac and which was probably also the basis of the original zodiac of the Babylonians and Greeks.[18] And thirdly, the star-based sidereal zodiac greatly reduces in importance the most essential feature of astrology itself, namely the basic Earth–Sun relationship and the four cardinal points of the compass as I described earlier.

'It is also worth remembering, that the constellations have never been the distinct, irresistible units that one might commonly suppose. Different cultures invariably use different stars to form different patterns in the sky and there are scarcely any which have been consistently interpreted as bearing the same, common resemblance from culture to culture, era to era. A good example of this is our own northern constellation of Ursa Major whose various sizes, boundaries and titles are legion in historical terms and which still retains numerous images in the West even today: the Plough, the Big Dipper, Charles' Wain, the Great Bear, and so on. Similar if not greater ambiguity surrounds the ancient constellations of the zodiac. Each culture invents different mnemonic tags and boundaries that best suit its agricultural, climatic, mythological and religious experiences.

'Indeed, it seems most unlikely that the majority of dull and obscure asterisms along the ecliptic circle were ever seen as fancied resemblances to anything at all. Occasionally, titles were awarded to particularly prominent stars that might later have given their names to areas of sky. The two bright stars that feature in the constellation of Gemini are a good example and would naturally be thought of as brothers or twins. But actual pictorial representation – joining up the dots like some tedious puzzle found in the back pages of a magazine – is a comparatively modern fixation. Certainly in all the available illustrations of the star groups found in Egyptian and Sumerian monuments there is no attempt to superimpose visual images on to the stars themselves, even when these are clearly listed, or in some cases drawn. An illustration to help with memory may appear alongside the stars or their names, but never actually upon them.[19]

'Ideas and knowledge were always transferred orally in antiquity. In fact it is perhaps not generally appreciated how widespread this practice was, particularly in the days before the invention of an alphabet and the simple convenience of pen and paper.[20] Remembering complex ideas through visual imagery was essential, and the rich symbolism of the zodiac is entirely consistent with such a tradition. The twelve precise divisions of the astrologer's zodiac are exclusively a product of the inclination of the Earth's equator to the plane of the ecliptic and the seasonal changes which arise as a consequence. If this frame of reference does shift with time in relation to the background of stars, it really doesn't matter. Astrologers continue to apply the old names like Aries, Taurus, etc., to the zodiac signs simply as a mnemonic device, enabling them to fix the character of each sign clearly, to remember it, and communicate it to others. The notion, therefore, that astrologers are somehow addicted to ancient and poetic fantasies, the constellations in the skies of classical Greece and Rome, with all their vagueness and irregularity, and upon which the entire credibility of modern astrology depends, is totally erroneous.

'Ptolemy in the second century AD states in the introduction to his great catalogue of stars, the *Almagest*, that he has not always kept to the constellation figures of his predecessors any more than they had always kept to theirs. The much earlier work of Hipparchus in the second century BC is clearly referred to here, since it was said that he in turn did exactly the same to the old catalogues on which his own were based.[21] Unlike other oft-quoted commentators of the period, such as Manilius, this is the attitude of an astronomer, not a poet or myth-maker, an attitude entirely consistent with our modern preference for a moving tropical zodiac – and is why our current ideas of how the constellations themselves first arose could actually be based on an entirely false premise. These mythical, it would also seem from your description, rather idle or insomnious ancestors of ours, gazing at the heavens and joining up the dots, have possibly never existed outside of the romantic notions of contemporary scholars and historians.

'Such ancient and largely nomadic peoples would, however, have been extremely interested in the passing of the seasons and in navigation, both by land and sea. They would have used individual stars as markers wherever applicable, changing these and their names from generation to generation as circumstances demanded. Pretty pictures were not a priority.

'In fact even if we wanted to, most of us would be hard-pressed indeed to form pictures of any kind in the stars. If you don't believe me, go out yourself, look at the constellation of the Ram and see if you can see a picture there. I can assure you that there is absolutely nothing resembling a Ram among its stars, or indeed any creature for that matter. But unfortunately the quaint theory of an astronomy born of the sleepless musings of primitive peoples is now enshrined in our history of science, and it seems cannot be questioned.

For artists, the pictures-in-the-sky notion has always remained an appealing one of course. Over the years, and as techniques of draughtsmanship became more and more refined, cosmographers and map makers of the Greek world embellished their works with detailed descriptions and drawings of the creatures and heroes which the poets had elevated to the skies, each painstakingly fitted into the vague, arbitrary arrangements of the stars, until by the time of Manilius in the first century AD we arrive at the absurd situation where Taurus the Bull has to be visualised rising backwards with one foreleg – lame we are told – bent double beneath its foreshortened, truncated body just in order to accommodate the grand illusion that one stage further.[22]

'Similar incredible contortions had to be undergone by the other signs as the drive for pictorial representation grew apace.

111

Ptolemy stood for some sanity when he reminded everyone about precession and the moving zodiac. But by then the pictures-in-the-sky idea had taken on a life of its own. Still greater elaborations continued into the Roman and Arab worlds. The trend, the fixation spread unchecked, even migrating into the astrological systems of other lands such as India and China, who already had their own totally different star names to contend with, and then through to the European Renaissance and the magnificent star maps of its artists and engravers: all very beautiful, but of no practical value to astrologers.

'Meanwhile, astronomers themselves, not astrologers, seem to be the ones most stuck in the past, adhering to the star patterns and shapes of ancient Greece and Rome, and of men and women who lived and died almost two thousand years ago. And if it is true that we can no longer change our constellations to fit the zodiac and the seasons, this is due entirely to the conservatism of astronomical science, rather than any absence of technical understanding among astrologers. The old zodiac of fixed stars can, in fact, be safely seen as little more than a relic, a fossil that, unchanging, is stuck in one particular frame of reference, of little use to anyone except perhaps modern cartographers who still use it to form some of their own constellation boundaries.

'So you see, there is nothing wrong with our zodiac. It is just as it always has been, a wonderful reflection of our planet's place in the solar system and its relationship with the Sun, which, in turn, receives the still greater fields present in our galaxy, and which bear directly on numerous chemical and electromagnetic functions which have absolutely nothing to do with irrelevant and largely non-existent fixed patterns of star shapes or figures.[23]

'The zodiac and the history of astrology is something that can be explored and discussed at great depth, and I hope here I have been able to give you some idea of the actual scope and complexity of a subject that is by no means as cut-and-dried an affair as many would imagine. Astrologers make use of the precession of the equinoxes. It is the very basis of their art. And if the constellations are ignored by most modern professionals, it is an omission entirely to their credit, and should not in any way be a source of criticism of astrology itself.'

Note: Occasionally you might encounter somebody who has

just read a newspaper article or seen something on TV that refers – and the headline doesn't change much over time – to the fact that the astrologer's zodiac has suddenly been rendered invalid due to the 'discovery' of a 13th sign. This is, in fact, a 'discovery' which is made regularly every few years. This salient lack of originality does not seem to deter many of astrology's detractors, however, and the attack will usually go along the lines of something like:

'What about the 13th sign, though? That throws the whole zodiac out, doesn't it? It shows how out of touch astrologers are with recent discoveries.'

Counter-attack: 'You are referring to the constellation of Orphiuchus, that's all – a particularly dull and barren area of the sky which has been designated as a constellation since the time of Ptolemy and which happens to run into the ecliptic. But it's not a zodiac sign. The astrologer's zodiac is a precise twelve-fold division of the ecliptic starting at the spring equinoctial point. It moves as that point moves over the centuries through the constellations. Ophiuchus, the Serpent-bearer, is just a group of scattered fixed stars that resembles nothing very much at all – and a very convenient constellation in fact, since just about any collection of disparate dots can be joined up to create a serpent. But it has nothing to do with the zodiac, and certainly doesn't throw anything out.'

Critique 6: New Planets

'Astrologers are said to welcome the discovery of three new planets beyond the orbit of Saturn. What seems strange, though, is that while they can insist that these have definite characteristics that aid in interpretation, they still maintain, in the same breath, that the astrology of antiquity was of an entirely competent standard – even though the charts were incomplete. How can the old astrology have been so fine and venerable without the knowledge of the new planets? How, then, could it work so well? And if it did work so well, why do astrologers today need to take the new planets into account at all? You either need them, or you don't.'

Combat: 'To admonish modern astrologers for using the new planets of Uranus, Neptune and Pluto in their charts while at the same time retaining the utmost respect for the work and traditions of antiquity, is rather like upbraiding the surgeon for using the latest equipment in the operating theatre alongside his traditional medical knowledge. For the surgeon, the long and venerable history of medicine remains of unquestionable value, but the work is improved by new methods and instruments and the success rate of medical operations is increased. Nor is the proven skill of doctors in the distant past, say an acupuncturist in ancient China, in any sense diminished for not having had access to the lasers, scanners and x-ray diagnoses of the twentieth century.

'Yes, the new planets are a great help. But the old astrologers, with their old charts still had it right, to the best of their ability – which was considerable, and all the more remarkable, perhaps, for having less than the full repertoire of planetary correlations to draw upon. Always, astrologers have done the best they can, using the best data available at the time; in this respect nothing has changed. Possibly that repertoire is still not yet complete.

'There is also a further point worth mentioning here, although it will only appeal to you if you are prepared to allow an element of evolution to enter your vision of the human psyche. Some astrologers feel that the discovery of the new planets may have coincided on each occasion with an expansion or change in both the material and psychological background of society itself. The new planets suit the modern world admirably. For, you must admit, our post-Newtonian person is a vastly different animal, caught in a vastly different universe to that of antiquity. The discovery of the new bodies might almost be seen as a necessity for astrologers who would otherwise be at a distinct disadvantage when trying to penetrate the complex character of the modern psyche.

'For example, Uranus came on the scene in 1781; about the time people began to harness mechanical force and social cohesion as a way of transforming society. This was marked by the Industrial Revolution, as well as the political revolutions in France and America. Neptune's discovery in 1846 seems to have coincided with the breakdown of spirit into rational intellect that accompanied Darwin, Marx and scientific reductionism, as well as the natural reaction to this in the Romantic period of philosophy, music and literature; while Pluto came along in 1930 together with the development of atomic physics, multinational plutocracies, the Wall Street crash and the awesome forces of power and potential destruction so typical of the present nuclear age.

'To some astrologers, though by no means all, none of this is coincidental, and is given added spice by the fact that the age in which each planet was discovered also seems to reflect the character pertaining to its respective counterpart in classical mythology. This parallelism is persuasive when viewed in terms of human consciousness and social change.

'Uranus and his cruel all-embracing authoritarianism, therefore, relates quite convincingly to the industrial and revolutionary eighteenth century. Neptune, god of the sea and the unconscious depths, adds his ethos in the nineteenth century with Romantic idealism and the great and illusory ego trip of atheism that swept like a vast tempestuous wave through Western society at that time. And then Pluto, the unforgiving, devastating god of the underworld, so obviously manifest in the atomic, plutocratic age, becomes quite readily the perfect *Zeitgeist* of our own troubled times.

'So, yes, it is just possible, and worth considering, that not only did the astrologers of antiquity have no knowledge of Uranus, Neptune and Pluto, but also no need for them either, simply because the vast majority of people at that time did not respond to the special character and special energy now identified with these bodies. Who knows, with time, there may be more planets yet to be discovered? If and when they come to light, however, you can be certain we will all be ready for the change, and ripe for it too.'

Note: Here you are showing astrology in the light of change and development. The impression should be that astrology is not static or fixed, but constantly evolving and, hopefully, improving with time.

There is, however, a further objection to the new planets, which your opponent might spring on you at any time: the breakdown of the mystical number seven. The attack itself could be something on these lines:

'The discovery of Uranus in 1781, and the subsequent revelations concerning other new major planets, not to mention numerous minor ones, has destroyed the sacred Law of Seven so precious to the ancient astrologers. If you include the Sun and the Moon, there were once just the seven bodies known to antiquity, and this fitted nicely into the whole chimera of correspondences: the seven days of the week, seven colours of the rainbow, and so on. Astrology must be rather embarrassed now this special number is no longer relevant.'

Note: The critique here is typical of those perpetrated by conventional historians when reviewing the history of astronomy. They do tend to develop these wild and, it seems, almost immovable notions about the effect science has had on astrology, without ever once bothering to ask astrologers themselves if these claims are valid. A little amusement blended with ironic indignation may awaken your opponents from their reverie.

Counter-attack: 'Of course it's relevant. There are still the seven naked eye components of the solar system; still the seven planets, just as there are still seven colours in the visible spectrum. The discovery of ultra-violet and infra-red light hasn't rendered the seven colours we still see with our eyes any the less complete or relevant, has it? Ask any artist or painter if it has. And in the same way the new planets beyond Saturn have not changed the uniqueness of the visible solar system.

'The number seven is also far from indispensable within the highly flexible and ever evolving system of astrology, which regards the numbers three, four and twelve as possessing at least equal significance.'

Critique 7: Conception

'While one must agree that conception and the bringing together of inherited characteristics is not the entire story regarding the making of an individual, it still seems unlikely that the moment of birth can be of any real importance in terms of character. It is simply the moment the baby emerges from the womb and takes on an independent existence free of the umbilical cord.

'The bulk of scientific experience still favours conception and the fusing of the genetic information of the parents as the true beginning of life. If astrology does have a claim to authenticity, it really would need to use this moment, and no other. To refuse to do so highlights the often reckless indifference shown by astrologers to the facts of life.'

Combat: 'Astrologers have, from time to time, endeavoured to find a formula for determining the moment of conception: the Pre-Natal Epoch, as it has been called. They did so not because they favoured conception as the beginning of the individual entity, but because they perceived conception as the beginning of each individual organic life, or the animal existence. This was something worthy of investigation in its own right.

'However, most astrologers through the ages have also shared in the conviction, common to many religious or mystical people, that the human being is something more than a mere animal. The stuff of life is seen as something external as well as something generated within the organic human entity. Life, or spirit, is part of the ambience, and makes its impression on us particularly at birth.

'The celebrated psychoanalyst C.G. Jung, perhaps one of the greatest independent minds of the last century, summed up this idea perfectly when he wrote that the psyche, or unconscious, is something in which the ego is contained, rather than the other way round, as is commonly supposed. He illustrated this nicely by remarking, with characteristic sparkle, that perhaps there are also some unenlightened fish who believe they contain the sea.[24] The pure geneticist is a little like these fish, believing that all individuals contain their own personal lives and consciousness – a singular entity that comes together at the moment of conception, exclusively a product of their genes.

'One thing that all world religions have in common is the basic affirmation of an individual entity that somehow operates independently of the physical body and which, in its own way, is part of a greater whole. Call it the Spirit, the Soul, the Divine Spark, give it whatever name you like, but such an entity is generally agreed to enter the body at the time of birth and to leave it at the time of death. Countless examples from religious scripture, anthropology, art and mythology confirm this as an essential component of our innate mystical identity. The words "breath" and "spirit" both have a common origin in our language, and mean the same thing in many cultures. The moment of birth is, as you have said, the start of individuality, the first breath of a unique life.

'Now, of course, not all astrologers adhere to this singularly spiritual approach. Agnostics are by no means rare in this profession. But all agree that the time of birth is still of paramount importance in terms of individual character. Projections to and from the birth chart in the form of progressed aspects and transits give us a good idea of how that individual life will unfold and develop in time, in other words, forecasting. This practice has confirmed the importance of the birth moment emphatically over the millennia that astrology has been practised. Statistical evidence, moreover, confirms the existence of a vital planetary relationship between parents and children at the moment of birth. For instance, it has been clearly demonstrated that if a particular planet is strongly placed in the chart of one or both the parents, then it is also likely to be significantly present in the charts of their children.[25]

'That is why, regardless of whether it is believed that the soul enters the body at birth or not, the astrologer has rightly always preferred the certainty of a well-recorded birth time to anything else, for unless we are working under modern laboratory conditions, a chart for conception can, for physiological reasons, obviously only ever be surmised, never verified, and these days no one within the serious astrological fraternity pays much attention to the old Pre-Natal Epoch formulae. Astrologers, on the whole, like to put things to the test. Unverifiable data is not accepted blindly and will be abandoned if found to be false or unworkable.

'As for the science of genetics, this addresses itself to inherited characteristics only, the animal body of the individual. If you agree with me that we are more than just animals, then you must award to the moment of birth, and the subsequent environmental influence of the first few months of breath, a place of importance, if not priority, in the formation of each human personality.'

Note: At this stage, and especially if you are dealing with an atheist, you are likely to be interrupted and told that we *are* animals. Our entire individuality is a result of genetic inheritance. Even our so-called moral status is nothing more than a sublimated instinct for the preservation of the species arising from countless millennia of habitual reflex and environmental conditioning. Man is a clod of earth: the naked ape syndrome.

Do not despair. Certainly do not be intimidated. There are one or two excellent counter-moves against this argument, the most notable of which includes the late Sir Fred Hoyle's remarkable research into genetics. Hoyle, not an astrologer it must be said, is widely regarded as being one of the twentieth century's greatest independent thinkers. A prominent astronomer, mathematician and astrophysicist, his inventive and independent mind led him along many avenues of speculation, including a mathematical investigation into the viability of life evolving from the primordial slime of planet Earth as is commonly supposed by the atheists.

The complexity of genetic material is something not generally appreciated by most of us. The odds against the right stuff being created through the random coupling of atoms and molecules, in fact the odds against even a single protein in a human cell being formed by chance and natural selection, are so great – according to Hoyle – as to be utterly and hopelessly impossible, given the present estimated age of the universe, let alone the much younger Earth.[26]

Taking an illustration directly from Hoyle himself and his readable book on the subject (see Suggested Reading List, page 217), you can counter any interruption at this stage by simply stating that the chances of the precursors of life, that is one simple protein being formed accidentally from random formations of organic molecules – as is supposed to have occurred in the swamps of our planet not too long ago – are about the same as a person, blindfolded, solving the Rubik Cube puzzle. If this hypothetical and extremely patient person were to make one random move every second, it would take about 1,350 billion years to get it right, or about 300 times the current estimated age of the Earth. This is, remember, equivalent to forming just *one* of the body's proteins by chance. The cells of the human body employ about 200,000 different types of protein. And although Hoyle's critics have questioned the minutia of some of his calculations, the basic thrust of his argument has still not been adequately refuted.

Incidentally, do not be confused by the results of the numerous 'organic soup' experiments that, repeated constantly over the years, have claimed to have created the basic building blocks of life under laboratory conditions. These experiments, in which an electric spark is passed through a mixture of various chemicals, do eventually produce organic molecules called amino acids. But these are still a long way short of protein molecules that can consist of complex arrangements of hundreds or in some cases thousands of amino acids. And although some proteins have been engineered in the laboratory, a spontaneous formation has never been observed, nor perhaps is it ever likely to be since every amino acid within any given protein has to be in just the right place and in just the right order to prevent the protein becoming a useless molecular heap. The odds against a successful protein forming by chance, therefore, let alone several thousand of these managing to come together to form a living cell are absolutely overwhelmingly impossible. In this respect, Hoyle has also left us with another characteristically entertaining analogy, stating that the chance that higher life forms might have emerged in this way is comparable with that of a tornado sweeping through a junk-yard and accidentally assembling a Boeing 747 from the materials therein.[27]

'In other words, the universe, currently estimated to have the ridiculously trivial age of between ten and twenty billion years, is hardly old enough to have even got started on the incredibly complex business of forming even the background material for life. Somebody, somewhere has not been getting their sums right: perhaps because to do so would take us to a stage where some kind of creative intelligence might become evident in the cosmos. In this respect, Hoyle has at least been courageous enough to consider such a thing. He determined that not only organic molecules but also sophisticated biological structures might well be present within the interstellar matter, a kind of obscuring dust in space which was previously thought to be ice crystals or silicates. Life could well pervade the entire cosmos.

When confronted with these rather startling mathematical realities, the standard textbook champions of Darwinian evolution look decidedly quaint by comparison as they rush us recklessly in the space of a few billion years all the way through from basic amino acid building blocks to the already amazingly complex single-celled creatures that inhabited the early oceans and then ultimately to human beings with the genius and creative intelligence of a Shakespeare, Mozart or an Einstein.

In fact, this possible restoration of the human race to a position of dignity in the universe has certainly proved traumatic for some, which is why Hoyle's work was never exactly flavour of the month among those who preferred, and still do prefer, to view their fellow human beings as brutal animals born of a remarkably gratuitous set of cosmic accidents. Perhaps it is time the scientific establishment altered their perspective – although it should not be imagined that such a drastic rethink on their part would lead to any great innovation. Far from it. It would simply result in an idea remarkably similar to what many of us call God.

Critique 8: Fatalism

'Although it is true that man is often the slave of his passions, astrology seems to assume that such passions are directly answerable to the planetary and stellar forces, or at least related to them by a common synchronised pattern. It seems that the astrologer is cleverly hedging bets with this doctrine. If some of the predictions work out, all so well and good and the astrologer is jolly clever. If some of them don't work out, then free will has entered the picture and the customer is jolly clever. Either way the astrologer retains credibility.

'This is unacceptable. The idea that even some aspects of the future are already fixed implies that all aspects must be fixed. In other words, how can some things be predestined, while others remain open to question? Either the future is knowable or it is not. Free will in modern astrology is therefore nothing more than a sham, a kind of safeguard, firstly against making a wrong prediction, and secondly against appearing dogmatic and unreasonable – and thus concealing the basically dogmatic and unreasonable nature of astrology itself.'

Combat: 'Your critique is a fair one, but labours under a certain misapprehension concerning the nature of astrological prediction. Let us agree, firstly, that we leave popular astrology out of the discussion and concentrate on the work of the experienced professional, for much of what you say may be true of the former, but certainly not of the latter.

'The day-to-day experiences of a professional astrologer are usually in accordance with those within similar counselling or advisory occupations: doctors, psychologists, dieticians, teachers, welfare or probation officers, and so on. All of these will tell you that they see people of greatly varying character in the course of their work. Some who pass through their hands will be positive, self-assertive individuals, able to motivate and help themselves; people so fiercely independent that their schooling, their social group or even their doctor's prognosis seem quite incidental to the lives they lead. Others, though, are entirely the victims of their own selfish desires and fears, so much so that their lives are predictable even to the untrained eye. These are the ones at the opposite end of the scale – sad, introverted souls with hardly any vestige of self-confidence or independent volition, people who seem helpless in their struggle against the "cruel world" and the environment that has shaped them so easily.

'These variations are typical of the human condition, even though the social and material background can be the same for those who succeed as for those who fail. Free will is a variable, in other words, not only from one person to the next, but also from one period of a person's life to the next. Its use in modern astrology is not a method of hedging bets, as you put it. It is part of the philosophy of flexibility and common sense with which the astrologer approaches each individual client until a reasonable picture has been formed of the degree of independence at work within that individual's personality.

'Ultimately, it is the goal of any counselling astrologer to strengthen this independence, to urge each client to accept the framework of the birth chart and the way it unfolds with time as a means to self-understanding and self-mastery.

'Certainly, events are not mapped out in advance! Nobody would wish for such a thing, least of all the astrologer. Nor does anyone in the field of serious astrology ever "see" events in the future as if in a crystal ball. And if the strange and largely unexplained phenomenon of precognition is a reality, then it is certainly not one upon which astrologers normally draw. Rather, the astrologer deals with practicalities, with the alternatives and potentialities within the birth chart and the psyche. He or she weighs up the evidence and draws some intelligent conclusions. These alone will form the basis of any forecast or any approach to counselling.'

Note: At this stage, a stubborn opponent may introduce an historical twist and remark that, even though what you say sounds fair enough, the modern notion of free will in astrology is still a relatively new feature. Modern astrology, your opponent may insist, is built on a foundation of medieval fatalism. In practice, the interruption may go something like this:

Interruption: 'All this modern free-will business is fair enough, but astrology has changed its tune compared to the old days. The soothsayers and almanac makers of, say, the sixteenth century exuded fatalism, and were laughed at even in their own times by intelligent people. Modern astrology may be safe enough with its new emphasis on freedom, but if the history and foundations of the subject are based on primitive determinism, how can you expect people to take you seriously today?'

Counter-attack: 'Market forces always have, and always will, cater for the weak-willed and superstitious among the population, regardless of whether you are promoting astrology, or the latest brand of toothpaste. So yes, to be sure, we do still have our fair share of fatalists, and our almanac makers as well. Pick up any newspaper or popular magazine and you'll find them in abundance. But by the same token, the judicious, thinking professional has also always existed, and a clear distinction between serious and pop astrology has been present in all periods of history, and especially among educated people, the notion of free will in astrology has always been a built-in fixture. The fact that this acceptance was rarely referred to by name actually indicates the extreme familiarity of the idea to all concerned. Free will in astrology was always a concept assumed or at the very least discussed privately in educated circles. Most often, however, it was taken for granted.

'To imagine otherwise would be seriously to underestimate the integrity of some of the most outstanding individuals and some of the greatest minds throughout history. You mentioned the sixteenth century. Astrology was popular then, yet it still possessed many levels of sophistication. Invariably it was a vital ingredient in the mental and spiritual make-up of the educated classes: men like Raleigh, for instance who, in his *History of the World,* insisted that the stars have sway over the bodily weaknesses only. A man with a choleric imbalance, Raleigh suggests, is naturally prone to the faults and excesses of the planet Mars, but the immortal part of each man can be free.[28] These ideas were as much the property of the Renaissance as they were of the Greek, Roman and Gothic cultures that preceded it. There is, for example, a similar kind of view in the writings of Thomas

Aquinas, who did not dispute the powers of the stars, but believed that they exert an influence on the "lower man" only.[29]

'By the same token it was realised that to function creatively within the framework of astrological forces, was a quality to which the best would always aspire. To know oneself, one's weaknesses and strengths, and then work with these to evolve and to grow at every available opportunity was the goal of the whole man, or whole woman. And, indeed, it is among the Elizabethans themselves that we can find some of the best illustrations of this principle. You may notice that it is the choleric, headstrong characters in the plays of Shakespeare, for instance, who always seem to bluster against what they mistakenly perceive as fatalism in the lives and institutions of those around them: "The fault, dear Brutus, is not in our stars, But in ourselves, that we are underlings," states the plotter in *Julius Caesar,* unaware of his own choleric imbalance. The scheming character of Edmund in *King Lear* is a further example of this kind of misguided belligerence. These are always the villains, the fools of the drama who have to learn the lessons of humility, realism and virtue. The Elizabethan stage bristles with such characters. Yet perversely, it is precisely the immature ravings of many of Shakespeare's villains, the hubris, egoism and overbearing pride of his tyrants that are cited today by otherwise quite perceptive commentators as indications of the playwright's supposedly anti-astrological stance.

'Nothing could be further from the truth. The informed audiences of the Elizabethan theatre would have understood the imbalance, the weaknesses and excesses of these figures, and would also have recognised in their invective against divination merely the profound imperfections of the characters themselves who, far from displaying independence, where simply showing themselves for what they were, the obstinate slaves of their own passions and, consequently, of their stars. Such invective was a device, a dramatic embellishment. Genuine free will was taken for granted as much in those times as any other but it was recognised as an attribute of the wise and virtuous, working within their own current limitations rather than the mere posture of the headstrong and vainglorious seeking to overturn the world for their own selfish ends. Lear was a man who "hath ever but slenderly known himself," says Regan in Shakespeare's masterpiece. The vanity and unrealistic defiance of those who cannot understand or rule themselves or their pride can only end in misfortune – in real life as much as in the stories and dramas of antiquity. Such was the often-obvious moral present in the old dramatic characters that we now miss or else totally misinterpret.

'Only rarely today, as little as then, do we ever see sober judgement triumphing over greed; ever see modesty and dignity triumphing over self-worship and cynicism. In that respect nothing much has changed. Just as always, the world is full of Edmunds, Caesars and Macbeths: everywhere from the hysterical financial markets of the big cities to the famine stricken battle zones of the developing world. Astrology is far from a cure for such universal ills, but it does help to draw back the veil a little. The rest is up to each of us and to the free will that we all possess, if only we are sensible enough to accommodate it within the laws of nature.'

Critique 9: Forced Births

'With the advance in modern obstetrics and the trend towards induced births, surely there must now be many more babies born during social hours rather than, say, at night. This must mean a lot more people being born with the Sun over the horizon than was the case in the old days. If astrology and things like the position of the Sun have any bearing on character, doesn't this trend somehow narrow the range of individual self-expression, one child to the next? More importantly, if astrology maintains subtle and special relationships as being discernible in the comparison of individual charts, say mother to child, then surely induced births interfere with the natural alignment of such factors?

'Taken one step further, if induced births invalidate the natural flow of things so much, how is it that we and our children are still, on balance, a fairly healthy and diverse lot? No one seems any the worse for the new trends. Isn't this all just one more blow to the validity of astrology and the importance it constantly assigns to non-essentials?'

Note: Although this argument seems to be pitched at a higher level than the corresponding one under sparring (see page 86), it is fundamentally still the same. Actually, it is surprising how often it crops up; surprising, too, the difficulty people find in reconciling induced births with natural astrology – whatever 'natural' astrology is supposed to be. It also seems that many of us are instinctively uneasy about artificial birth practices – and with good reason it would seem in the light of the research by Michel Gauquelin.[30]

Combat: 'Yes, it is true that many more births now take place during what could be called office hours. For example, it has been estimated that there are almost a quarter fewer births registered on the inconvenient day of Sunday than on normal working days, and Christmas, too, is an unpopular time for having your baby. Fewer births are allowed then, with consequently a sudden escalation in the number directly after Boxing Day.[31]

'As to any possible artificial effect through more births during the daylight hours, this will be negligible. The position of the Sun in the chart, which relates to the cycle of the day, of course, is only one factor among many which can differentiate between personalities, child to child. As for horoscopic relationships between parent and child, generally it has always been thought that, even in those cases where these are not evident in a comparison of the charts, that any given birth time has always been the right time for that individual, regardless of how bizarre the circumstances surrounding the birth may have been. Indeed, until only quite recently, astrologers have been settled and content with this position, that is until the work of the French statistician and psychologist Michel Gauquelin revealed quite clearly that there is an important astrological link between parents and their offspring that is significantly damaged by the practice of induced births.

'During his long and painstaking research, initially calculating and studying by hand over fifteen thousand parent–child relationships, or thirty thousand charts in all, remarkable in the age before the widespread availability of computers, Gauquelin discovered that if a particular planet is strongly placed – that is if it is culminating or rising in the chart of a parent, mother or father – then there is a strong chance that it will also feature prominently in the chart of the child. A further survey, covering a massive one hundred thousand births in all, confirmed this relationship beyond doubt. This link appears far more often than chance would allow and is, in statistical jargon, highly significant.[32]

'Interestingly enough, this relationship disappears entirely when cases of induced birth are examined. Research is not yet comprehensive enough to know whether or not other astrological factors, cross aspects for example, may compensate whenever Gauquelin's shared-planets feature is absent, but nevertheless, the existing conclusions are clear: that the natural moment of birth is, as Gauquelin put it, a precious indicator of hereditary temperament.

'This subtle link of heredity and character would be of immense importance in communication and understanding between the child and its parents in later life and would, presumably, aid greatly in the process of ethical and moral education. Its absence, on the other hand, could have far reaching social effects of which we are perhaps only just beginning to see evidence, since the fashion for controlled technical deliveries, with all the attendant paraphernalia of machines, surgical tools and pain-killing drugs, has only been prevalent since about the 1960s.'

Note: Gauquelin's findings may well add a new and unsettling dimension to the recent practice of surrogate motherhood, where an infertile couple can contract the pregnancy out, as it were, to another woman. Also relevant, would be the sperm bank business, where a woman can choose a father for her child via artificial insemination, a father with probably quite excellent genetic credentials but one whom the child itself will never know. One can only wonder at what peculiar astrological concoctions must result from such births.

Undoubtedly, in the light of what we now know of parent–child relationships in astrology, natural childbirth is to be recommended and encouraged as perhaps one of the best possible means of ensuring parent–child rapport. The statistical work has been replicated, and although it does have its detractors – as does all statistical work in astrology, and some of which it has to be said is quite bizarre – there should no longer be any serious doubt that such an astrological and hereditary link exists when nature is allowed to take her course.

Yet, having said this, and despite the findings of Gauquelin, most astrologers still adhere to the conviction that any set of circumstances, and any time of birth, is always the right one: the one that is necessary for the individual concerned. And for some, the suspicion that we might be fostering a generation totally out of step with its forebears is taken – admittedly with a certain degree of sadness – to be perhaps a necessary phase of our collective evolution, the mechanical nature of modern birth and even surrogacy as being simply the means to that end.

Before finishing, there is just one more point worth mentioning. Gauquelin's research can now be seen as a persuasive and cogent factor in terms of the overall credibility of astrology, since it seems unlikely that nature would have organised, no matter how blindly, such a link within families if planetary bodies had no influence or importance in terms of organic life here on Earth. This research was further reinforced by Gauquelin when he discovered that the planetary relationship, parent to child, was enhanced during times of increased activity in the Earth's geomagnetic field – due, in turn, to ionised particles emanating from the Sun: evidences of a clear astronomical link.

You can employ these points at any time in your debate as a general confirmation of astrology's validity and practical relevance in daily affairs. But make sure you thoroughly understand the research first, and the views of its critics. Remember also, that it is – in the opinion of some astrologers – unwise to use statistical findings to defend astrology at all because, if true, these would ultimately constitute a negation of free will. See the reading list at the end of this book (page 217) for the best way of gaining access to Gauquelin's work, and you will find more about the usefulness or otherwise of statistical evidence on pages 183–97.

Critique 10: Paganism

'Astrology is a cult, one which has dangerous pretensions towards being a religion. It encourages people to abandon the ways of the true God who has endowed mankind with free will and sent his son Jesus to show us the means and the way of salvation through worship and good works. Astrology seeks to inculcate a sense of fatalism and selfishness in people. It is a primitive pagan belief, based on a pantheon of often cruel and wicked gods who, according to classical sources, committed all sorts of repugnant crimes, from incest to murder, who celebrated their powers by laughing at the misfortunes of the lame or the poor or by stirring up mischief, war and strife between mortals for their own entertainment and gratification.

'The true Christian virtues of charity, universal love and humility are foreign to such gods. Their projection through the superstitions of astrology is the work of the Devil, essentially evil and totally incompatible with the lives of decent men and women in any civilised country.'

Note: This may sound a little extreme – and indeed it is. Nevertheless, it typifies a criticism you might encounter at times, especially if you are teaching astrology locally, or hoping to deliver a talk or series of lectures on the subject. You should bear in mind that although this is not, as such, a successful attack against astrology, to an opponent of this kind it may seem tantamount to one, and you will of course want to treat it with respect.

Religions of all kinds are based on many intangible propositions as is astrology itself, so you can perhaps sympathise with a person who wishes to discuss and debate ideas of this kind. Our particularly vitriolic opponent here, however, is presumed to be a practising Christian, since of all the great world religions, Christianity at the present time is perhaps the only one to be overtly hostile to astrology.

Many representatives of Christianity, especially those belonging to the more recent Protestant creeds, including Quakers or Baptist for example, might feel that the pagan deities, Jupiter, Saturn, etc., are looked upon by astrologers as in some sense real external beings, and that credence in these can undermine Christian morality if taken in any way seriously. The best way to tackle such an antagonist is to begin by genuinely complimenting Christianity. Show your open-mindedness and your willingness to consider all beliefs: in other words, to display the kind of tolerance and sobriety that he or she may be lacking.

Combat: 'Christianity at its best is a highly advanced religion, of course: a monotheism being able to synthesise many disparate and opposing qualities into one Great Being. It brings all the old gods together in one God, and is therefore well suited to the modern mind with its penchant for clarity and economy of ideas.

'Throughout history, moreover, astrology and its related subjects of mathematics, architecture, agriculture and the calendar, have enjoyed a prominent position in Christianity, not only as outward symbol, but also in the inner workings, sacraments, festivals, commissions and politics of the Church itself. Much of this was lost with the Reformation, when astrology was mistakenly associated with witchcraft and magic. It is from this time that the hostility or, at best, grim indifference towards astrology by those of the Christian faith originates.

'The extent of orthodox feeling in those times must never be underestimated; those who even today are only too ready to condemn others as evil would do well to remember the outcome of such righteous indignation. Estimated figures for the number of witch killings from the fifteenth to the seventeenth centuries run to a staggering six million.[33] Yet despite this attempted purge of the old ways, all branches of Christianity at the present time still contain, by their essential nature, much that is germane to the sacred mystery of the early Roman Church and therefore, it may surprise you, to astrology as well. To understand this, perhaps we should recall and examine in some detail the nature of early Christianity.

'It is now generally assumed that the early Church was founded upon three main elements: firstly Judaism; secondly the story of Christ; and finally Neo-Platonism and the mystery cults of the Near East. All these rich branches of study, devotion and inspiration converged during the first and second centuries AD. They were naturally embodied in the structure of early Roman Christianity, and became in time the foundation of the many diverse Christian creeds we know and recognise today.

'Regarding the first source, Judaism and the sacred history upon which Christianity is founded, we find ample evidence for the use of astrology in the Old Testament era. Indeed, the mysteries residing in the Kabalah are essentially mystical and astrological in nature, and stem directly from the ancient Jewish occult tradition. To somehow imagine that astrology and magic were exclusively the property of the Tower of Babel and foreign to Judaism is a serious error, therefore, and one which does not stand up to even the most basic level of historical investigation.

'The second source, the story of Christ in the New Testament of the Bible, fulfils many of the prophecies of the Old Testament, and also echoes numerous features found there. For example, the story of Jonah and the whale in the Old Testament becomes the story of the resurrection in the New. This parallelism has been treated extensively, and forms one of the commonplaces of Christian iconography and biblical scholarship. In addition to this, the historical figure of Jesus seems to have become embellished with many of the attributes of the mythical Sun god heroes of the Greeks or the Middle East such as Dionysus, Orpheus or Mithras, whose death and resurrection were bound up inextricably with the seasons and the festivals that marked their passing. Ceremonies such as baptism, and the biblical symbolism of the cave or the cross are also thought to be derived from such sources. Orpheus or Bacchus are to be found in the unfortunate position of hanging from the cross centuries before our own Christ was depicted in this way, while the same number symbolism and the numerological predominance of twelve and four is to be found as much in the Old Testament as in the New – a continuous reference to the four quarters of heaven, the zodiac and to all those earlier mystery religions that celebrated astrology. Moreover, the zoomorphic or animal forms pertaining to the four Evangelists are essentially zodiacal in origin. The evidence for this, found in Gothic and Renaissance architecture throughout Europe, is indisputable.[34]

'The third main source of Christian doctrine, the traditional Greek philosophies and the later Neo-Platonism of the Roman scholars, constituted the mainstream intellectual background of the Roman and Greek world at the time of the foundation and consolidation of the Church around the first and second centuries AD. Ideas such as the Kingdom of Heaven, the Trinity, the Chain of Being from mineral through vegetable, through animal, through man, the angels and ultimately God; the idea of a distinct and indestructible soul for each person; of Purgatory; of the Unmoved Mover as God: all these are essential to Neo-Platonism or earlier Greek thought and religion. The leading figures of the early Church, Ambrose, Jerome, Augustine, all existed within this intellectual framework – this same great continuum of ideas. It is impossible to treat the lives of such men in isolation to the vast body of mystical and astrological doctrine common to the classical world at that time. Much of this was modelled on Neo-Platonism, and was consequently rooted in the ideas of the much earlier Pythagoreans, whose inspiration, in turn, can be traced to the ancient religions of Egypt and Sumeria.[35]

'Such was the basic chemistry at work in the building of the early Christian Church, although there were of course many additional ingredients. It is known, for example, that the Greeks influenced later Jewish writers, and these writings in turn influenced the teachings of Jesus, making the overall picture a complex one. Yet astrological symbolism was one of the few common elements present in each of these varied sources, shared and understood by all.

'As we know, within the Roman world as much as in that of the Greeks or Egyptians, the understanding of the heavens remained of great practical importance: indispensable to navigation and to the fixing of the calendar, both for civil and for devotional purposes. This was the outer manifestation of the deeper, inner cosmic mystery that remained with the authority of the Church throughout the Middle Ages and Renaissance, and which can be discovered in the architecture, sculpture and literature of the times.[36] Among the Romanesque style of church architecture, carvings and paintings, we find numerous representations of astrological symbolism: in the Labours of the Months and their parallels with the signs of the zodiac, for example. Pictorial associations of this kind can even be traced right back to Byzantine times in mosaic and relief carvings.

'Throughout the subsequent centuries such ideas became endemic to both the Church and the lay community alike, both East and West. With time this natural partnership of astrological mysticism and Christianity migrates through into Gothic symbolism, buildings, pavements and carvings. The roundels in Canterbury Cathedral are a good example. Almost every church and cathedral contains similar items, be it on the grand scale of architectural proportion and stained glass, as at Chartres, or in the humble carvings on village pulpits and fonts. The four Evangelists with their zoomorphic and astrological symbolism, Piscean and Taurean imagery reminding us of the esoteric, solar Christ and the Logos respectively – all these are to be found consistently in places of Christian worship.[37]

'Rather than simply being seen as a pagan remnant obstinately holding on to the crevices of Christian iconography, therefore, astrological representation in religious art and architecture was always recognised as a working reality. Its presence even increases during the Middle Ages and still later with the Renaissance and the Humanist movement in Italy, a movement begun by Petrach and later developed by Marsilo Ficino under the patronage of the Medicis, and, therefore, of the Pope and the Church itself. The founders of this movement deliberately set out to blend paganism and Christianity, adding the ideas of Dante, Cicero, Virgil and Plotinus to the teachings of Christ, to produce a vast coherent system that inspired whole generations of religious thought and artistic genius – men such as Raphael, Michelangelo, Botticelli, and many, many more. In the devotional as well as the secular work of these artists, astrological, biblical and Neo-Platonic symbolism are to be found extensively and quite happily side by side. All owe their ideas to the Humanists, inspired by astrology.

'On a more practical day-to-day level, astrology was always an essential component of Renaissance court life, and to military, civil and ecclesiastical affairs. Popes employed astrologers for advice on just about anything from political or military campaigning, to the most propitious time for a coronation or consistory. In privately commissioned art, meanwhile, astrological themes featuring the pagan divinities were commonplace in private apartments and chapels. Michelangelo's ceiling frescoes in the Sistine Chapel, and Raphael's decoration of the papal apartments of the Vatican, each combines theological programmes with classical humanist features. None of this was considered to be in the least bit incompatible with a sense of Christian devotion and piety, which was so prevalent in those times.

'Moreover, the Christian orthodoxy of such astrologically committed families as the Medicis is obvious and sincere – and can clearly be perceived in the way in which, when worldly success came, in whatever form, military or civil, it was to God alone that a votive painting or carving was dedicated, not to the pagan gods. For although the planets might have indicated the unfolding of events, it was the Great Spirit behind them that ultimately shaped the world and the lives of its people. Examples of this abound at the time of the Church's zenith. For instance, above the tomb of the wealthy fifteenth-century banker Agostino Chigi, in the church of St Maria del Popolo in Rome, is a cupola, by Raphael, in which the planets are depicted. Over each one there floats an angel, while at the summit, as in a Byzantine church, is seen the image of the Almighty. So God is recognised by all as the ultimate ruler, the Unmoved Mover of the angels, the planets over which they have dominion, and therefore of humankind itself.[38]

'In the Protestant countries of northern Europe, meanwhile, Astrology's intimate relationship with Christianity even survived the Reformation. Ideas such as the great Chain of Being and the angelic hierarchies pertaining to the planetary spheres, were a common mental currency to those living in the Tudor and Elizabethan era. Here, as elsewhere, Christian ideology blended easily with the rapidly evolving ideas of the cosmos and its structure, and owed as much to the newly discovered teachings of the *Timaeus* of Plato as to the New Testament. There was, moreover, absolutely no contradiction, no dichotomy in the philosophy of the Church regarding the blending of astrology and Christianity. Even during the worst excesses of the dissolution of the monasteries in England during the reign of Henry VIII astrological themes continued to flourish.

'It is also important to remember that never, at any time, were the planets seen as living devotional figures or pagan deities to be worshipped in place of the Holy Trinity. Rather they were considered to be visible aspects of the divine will. For, as Jung has pointed out, astrology represented the summation of the psychological knowledge of antiquity.[39] The planets were regarded each as a separate psychic force, each a representational component of human nature set within the dynamic cosmic order of God.

'The later rejection of astrology in northern Europe came mainly from secular quarters, and not initially from within the Protestant Church. And if any debate did ever arise among churchmen concerning astrology, it was always of the traditional kind to be found in Augustine and, later, Aquinas, which centred on the nature of free will – discussions that are still going on today among astrologers and theologians alike. The actual breakdown of the peaceful coexistence between Christianity and astrology came, in fact, only as late as the seventeenth century with the rise of Puritanism, the witch hunts and the slightly more positive spirit of the Enlightenment. Then as much as now it was thought prudent to negate much of the ritual, adornment and magical connotations of the old Church and, along with this, much of the fatalistic doctrine of Catholicism and early Protestantism in favour of individual integrity and independence of worship. In this climate, astrology became wrongly associated with medieval repression and gloom even more than it had been with the Tower of Babel. The current unrest felt by Christians of all denominations towards astrology therefore owes its origins as much to the rising merchant classes of the seventeenth century, with their increased material and secular power, as it does to any illusory pagan or heathen genealogy.'

Note: The argument so far may be sufficient to satisfy those of the Catholic denomination, and possibly even a moderate Protestant. If you are faced with a fundamentalist, you may not fare so well. You have already made a rather disturbing observation here, implying that when a religion rejects its ceremony and much of its mysticism, as has recently happened in Christianity, then obviously something as integral as astrology will tend to share the same fate until, perhaps, a new cycle of fresh devotional experience starts the whole process going again.

This subtle presence of mysticism, almost waiting in the wings for its reunion with religious culture in the West, is perhaps another reason for the unease and even horror with which astrology may be viewed in certain quarters. Ultimately, in this case, reason or temperance on your part will be to no avail, and you will simply have to agree to disagree with your opponent. Remain confident, calm and detached, the most impressive defence of all in this kind of highly charged emotional situation – and above all respectful.

Sometimes, however you might be confronted by an opponent who will insist on quoting from the Bible to prove that astrology is un-Christian. There are only a handful of such quotations that refer directly to astrology, and these are actually from the Old Testament. An example would be from Isaiah: 'God is both the Creator and sovereign Ruler of the heavens; people are therefore to trust and fear Him – not what He has made.' What these passages all seem to have in common, however, is that they simply warn us of the superiority of God to the works of astrologers, and that whatever predictive power astrology has, it is utterly eclipsed by the power of the Lord who rules all things. Fair enough! The acknowledgement of a universal force greater than the individual self is actually something upon which all astrologers – or at least all professionals in the field – would probably agree without reservation. You can convey this to your opponent and stress the fact that humility, whether Christian or otherwise, is an accepted working principle of all serious astrological work.

Critique 11: Influence

'In ancient times, the planets and stars were thought to be important because they were associated with the gods who dwelt supposedly in the heavens. The vast distances of the planets and stars were not then understood, and it was natural to infer that they were connected in some sense with the world below. Now that we can calculate and comprehend astronomical distances, and realise how infinitesimally small are the gravitational and other effects exerted on the Earth by the far off planets, and even more remote stars, there is no longer any logical or rational foundation whatsoever for assuming the existence of any kind of influence from astronomical bodies. In short, the basic astrological tenet that the affairs of people are affected by extraterrestrial forces is not only scientifically groundless, but also wholly preposterous – as has been clearly demonstrated by studies undertaken with astrologers themselves.

'It is perhaps comforting for certain people to believe that their destinies are in some sense predetermined by mysterious astral forces beyond their control, but in truth we must all face up to the fact that such forces are non-existent. Our lives and our futures lie with ourselves alone, and not in the minute flickerings of distant starlight.'

Combat: 'Putting astrology to one side for just a moment, you seem to be unaware of the vast amount of scientific research and concrete evidence supporting the existence of numerous fields and forces of cosmic origin which, despite their subtlety, have been demonstrated to have influence and effects right here on Earth and upon the very biological processes of living things, including ourselves.

'You also seem to think that distances are the only criteria for judging or supposing influences to exist. This, typified by the inverse square law, may well be true for the force of gravitation – but even this is open to question when dealing with fundamental biological principles and the microscopic world on which all life depends. Here, in fact, distance is not especially significant.

'I can go over some of these recent developments, just briefly, to give you some idea of the progress and scope of current experimentation and its results. I am not suggesting that any of these will provide you with a definitive explanation for why astrology works, but only that current research does at least demonstrate how changes in subtle gravitational or electromagnetic fields can affect us, and especially during the early stages of life and shortly after birth. The best place to start is with the Sun. This is by far the most important body in the universe, as far as you and I are concerned. The Sun actually loses mass at the rate of four million tons per second, through immense internal atomic processes that are still far from fully understood. The Sun is a complex body of many different fields, waves and emanations. Apart from the obvious ones of heat and light, the most notable of these is the radiation associated with what is called the solar wind, a constant steam of ionised particles emanating from the Sun, also related in intensity to the phenomena of sunspots and the effect these have on the all-important magnetosphere surrounding the Earth. The magnetosphere serves as a shield in near space, protecting us from harmful radiation of this kind but it also fluctuates continually due to the strength of the solar wind.

'For centuries now, scientists have been aware of an eleven-year sunspot cycle. Sunspots are storms on the surface of the sun, observed darkened areas that appear in sharp relief against the brighter photosphere surrounding them. Their presence contributes to an attendant increase in the solar wind which then interacts with the magnetic field of the Earth causing the spectacular display of the northern lights, for instance, as well as producing disturbances to radio transmissions.

'We are now aware of numerous secondary cycles that are related to this eleven-year solar cycle and to fluctuations within the protective geomagnetic field of the Earth caused by tidal effects of the Moon and other planets. In other words every body within the solar system can contribute in some way to the variations in the local geomagnetic field of the Earth. I will explain the implications of this for the internal chemistry of the human body in just a moment. But suffice to say that in recent times it has become apparent that many biological organisms, including ourselves, can detect and respond to even minute changes in the geomagnetic field of our planet.

'When looking to the origins of these discoveries, we should firstly consider the pioneering work of the electrical engineer John Nelson – a radio propagation specialist for RCA Corporation in the middle of the last century – who demonstrated that both the weather and the quality of radio transmissions were affected indirectly by distant storms on the photosphere of the Sun, which in turn seemed to be affected by the angular relationships of the other bodies in the solar system. Nelson based his work on the traditional astrologer's aspects – angular relationships between the planets – but aspects as viewed from the Sun instead of from the Earth.[40] Although his work has been criticised owing to ambiguity in his system of measurement, later researchers took up his ideas and refined them, and NASA had no scruples about adapting his methods for predicting possible levels of radiation during the manned Apollo missions to the Moon during the 1960s and 1970s.

'In a purely scientific sense, however, and although the exact cause of the solar sunspot cycle and the resulting increases in the solar wind that emanates from it is still unknown, once we consider the phenomenon of solar activity and its effects on the geomagnetic field of the Earth, we must automatically draw in the Moon and the planets themselves. Although the gravitational pull of these bodies is weak, it is still thought to be significant due to a phenomenon called resonance, in which small force fields can produce large reactions through a unique tidal influence on the magnetosphere of the Earth. In addition to this, the gravitational forces stemming from the other planets are able to exert an influence on the Sun by helping it to shift around the common centre of mass of the solar system.[41] Despite its vastly greater mass compared with the other bodies in the solar system, the Sun accounts for only two per cent of the system's angular momentum, the rest resides in the planets. It seems reasonable, therefore, to expect that this force can be transferred to the Sun's surface, contributing to vortices, solar storms, and eventually those important magnetic disturbances in the Earth's atmosphere. There are, and have been, many models for such a mechanism, one of which relates to the movements of Neptune and Jupiter.[42]

'Changes in the Earth's magnetic field are important, and it is rapidly becoming apparent just how greatly these can effect the internal chemistry of life itself. Modern research has now demonstrated numerous direct and indirect connections at the biochemical level, such as changes in the behaviour of blood cells, which can in turn be related to incidence of heart failure and strokes, while cycles in diseases such as bronchitis and epilepsy seem, again, to be related in part to electrical changes in the Earth's atmosphere and therefore to changes in the original solar cycle.[43] Variations in solar radiation of this kind are also associated with what are called extra low frequency waves which have been found to predominate at peaks of industrial or traffic accidents and which have also been demonstrated to be present during periods of increased suicides or depressions.[44]

'When seeking a direct mechanism for just how electromagnetic radiation affects the physiological process, the pineal gland appears to be the most promising candidate. The interaction of the pineal gland with the geomagnetic field and its extreme sensitivity to fluctuations within this field have been studied extensively in recent times. This highly important component of the endocrine system produces various vital hormonal secretions such as melatonin, which in turn help regulate other vital endocrine glands situated nearby such as the pituitary and hypothalamus – thereby having control over everything from sleep and frequency of dreaming to the production of blood glucose, skin pigmentation, growth hormones, menstruation and the sex drive – and so ultimately the behaviour and the well-being of the individual concerned.[45] The hypothalamus, meanwhile – sometimes referred to as the master gland – has an input into the nervous system and affects those parts of the brain that help control our moods and motivational states.

Melatonin within the pineal gland is stimulated by darkness and inhibited by light – and so clearly related to the diurnal and seasonal cycles and the radiation from the Sun.[46] The pineal also plays a significantly vital role immediately after birth and during the first few days of life.[47] Additional sources of electromagnetic radiation can also affect the pineal during these critical early days: a period which has always been of special interest to astrologers, forming the basis of much of their forecasting. And in this context, there is further evidence that influences of this kind can produce a kind of pre-programing effect on the new-born infant that has ongoing consequences later in life by actually affecting the neural activity of the developing foetus, as well.[48]

The fact that melatonin production is influenced by other sources of electromagnetic radiation, including ambient Earth-strength magnetic fields, and that these have been linked to a wide range of physiological and psychological complaints later in life such as reproductive irregularities and depression, has even led some health professionals to re-assess the acceptable degree of exposure of new-born infants to strong light and other electromagnetic fields in the vicinity shortly after birth.[49] When considering electromagnetic radiation as a whole, moreover, one has to automatically consider the relationship of the Earth itself to the Sun and to the other fields present within the space around our planet. Not only the length of day, but also the geomagnetic field of the Earth varies by season and both are associated with changes in melatonin excretion, with observable peaks occurring in June and November. The solar wind, itself, meanwhile may also have a part to play in this intricate network of fields that affect the production of melatonin – with observable troughs occurring at the solstices and peaks at the equinoxes.[50] In this context, remember that the astrologer's zodiac in based on the equinoctial points and the seasons. So the network of connections is as intricate as it is real. And incidentally, if you have any doubts about the strength of these electromagnetic fluctuations in the Earth's atmosphere, be advised that it can be so strong in certain places at certain times as to completely shut down major power stations.

'1 think that we have adequately demonstrated the importance of seasonal and diurnal cycles on the welfare of people on Earth and that these are directly affected by the relationship of the Earth to the Sun. But what about the Moon?

'It is the Moon which has perhaps the most obvious, visible influence on our environment, from the ocean tides to the growth of plants, but there are many other subtle effects on organic structures that can be traced to the influence of this body – on animal and marine life, for instance. There is the well-known experiment in which oysters, when removed from a coastal laboratory to another location inland, quickly adjusted their feeding cycle to fit in with the timetable of tides for their new location, even though far from the sea and carefully screened in laboratory conditions from all external light sources. The oysters, regardless of their own internal clocks, were responding anew to something associated with the Moon's presence, even though the gravitational or magnetic influence of the Moon itself is considered minute.[51]

'Those critical of these findings often labour this last point. They say, for example, that the magnetic fluctuation of a typical household appliance is far greater than anything the Moon might be able to exert upon us. This, however, is true only at very close quarters. Move a short distance away from the offending object and the magnetic variations of the Moon become superior once again. The frequencies involved are also vastly different and could arguably be distinguished easily by living organisms. The effects of the lunar body are clearly evident everywhere in nature, and the gravitational force, under certain circumstances can be awesome – sufficient, for example, to shift one hundred billion tons of water out of the Bay of Fundy in Canada twice daily. Taking into account that we are all made up of around three-quarters water, the Moon is certainly an object which cannot be ignored when seeking a mechanism for possible influence.

'The breeding cycles of many creatures, including *homo sapiens,* clearly correspond to the cycles of the Moon. The length of the female menstrual cycle, averaging twenty-eight days, is identical to the synodic period of the Moon. There have also been many convincing studies of crime and mental disorder that suggest a variation in intensity running directly parallel with the lunar cycle.[52] (See also some studies mentioned in Chapter 12). Meanwhile, experiments with trees show marked fluctuations in electrical potential resulting from such subtle influences as the twenty-four hour solar rhythm, the twenty-five hour lunar rhythm, and a lunar cycle related to the phases of the Moon, reaching a peak when the full Moon passes directly overhead.[53]

Whenever experiments on the human bio-electrical field have been practicable, it has also been demonstrated that the electrical potential between the head and the chest clearly changes with the lunar phase.

'This subtle bio-electrical field that permeates and surrounds the bodies of all living things, including ourselves of course, has been the subject of greatly increased research in recent times, from a handful of studies in the middle part of the last century to over a thousand published each year at present. What we are talking about here exists – make no mistake about that – and, like the Earth's magnetic field, it is open to the smallest disturbances and influences. For instance, there is now a growing body of work that suggests that changes in geomagnetic and other ambient radiation can have a dramatic effect on the temporal lobes of the brain, producing subjective experiences and altered states of consciousness and emotions in humans.[54] Seasonal as well as diurnal variations in these fields are well documented.

'Still considering the Moon, the oxygen consumption of plants has been shown to relate to the lunar phases and to the lunar day, while the natural affinity between body fluids and the Moon is revealed by statistical research on the frequency of excessive haemorrhaging after surgical operations at particular phases of the lunar cycle.[55] It is also worth considering that apart from the direct effects attributable to the Moon, the lunar body also occasionally blocks off solar radiation to the Earth, or also combines with that particular source of influence in a way similar to the Moon's interaction with the solar body in producing spring or neap tides. Satellite measurements have shown this quite clearly.[56]

'Once you have established these relationships, all kinds of indirect ones become apparent until it becomes inescapably obvious that we are immersed in a vast network of fields and interactions. Nothing, least of all humans, can be viewed in isolation. Modern scientific research thoroughly endorses the existence of subtle life-fields in which all things share. Experiments really too numerous to mention here have isolated such fields in plants, animals and people, all of which respond to the greater cosmic stimuli of both the solar and galactic systems alike.[57]

'If you take the time to study these findings, I think you'll agree that the evidence for this organic life-field, and its receptivity to astronomical phenomena is quite substantial and impressive. However, it is when we start to look at direct planetary influences that things really start to get interesting. Apart from the regulating effect they have on electromagnetic disturbances on the Sun, experiments have shown that some direct form of electromagnetic radiation from these bodies does reach us on Earth and can, moreover, have observable effects, for example in relation to the metals over which each planet traditionally has a correspondence or rulership.

'Experiments in which metal salts are mixed and suspended in solutions, and which allow the rates of precipitation of these metals to be recorded and measured on to filter papers, clearly show a correlation to the angular positions of the planets traditionally associated with each metal. For example, suspend silver in a solution containing iron and then wait for a conjunction of the Moon and Mars. At the time of conjunction, the silver alters its rate of precipitation. Three quarters of an hour after the conjunction, the precipitation continues as normal. The Moon has always been associated with silver, as has Mars with iron. Similar results were obtained with the movements of Saturn and the metal lead.[58]

'These metals occur in small though vitally important quantities within the human body. Iron, for instance, is an essential ingredient of haemoglobin. We actually "breathe" through an iron compound in our blood. Iron is also an important agent in the synthesis of chemicals by the all-important pineal gland mentioned earlier. Copper, ruled by Venus, is also vital to the healthy functioning of the human organism, particularly the female, and particularly during pregnancy. It therefore also has a bearing on the well-being of the new-born infant. This in turn has numerous far-reaching physiological implications, since our bodies consist largely of suspended salts, solutions of organic material and water. Subtle concentrates of these metals tend, moreover, to settle in those parts of the body traditionally linked to the planets themselves. Lead, for example, has always been the metal of Saturn, and Saturn has traditionally always ruled the skeletal frame. We now know thanks to scientific analysis that lead in the human body is, indeed, to be found mostly in the bones.[59]

'The current state of the art in molecular biology and particle physics tells us that the human body and mind are far from the solid structures one might imagine. They are in fact an almost inconceivably vast collection of chemical and genetic intricacies held together by subtle atomic, electrical and magnetic fields. These fields are inseparable from our environment, from the atomic, electrical and magnetic matrix of everything around us, from the everyday objects here at this moment right up to the Sun and planets themselves. Action in one infers reaction in others – to varying degrees, to be sure – but all are interconnected in the best mystical tradition, something that is well understood by many of the foremost minds in today's scientific world community.[60]

'On a more concrete level, what may well turn out to be direct planetary influences on the mind and body have been detected through statistical research, the most successful of which is the work produced in the last century by the French psychologist Michel Gauquelin. Gauquelin located a firm and definite relationship between eminent men and women in various professions and the strength of planets such as Mars and Jupiter in their birth charts.[61]

'This requires some explanation. In astrological terms, a planet is considered strong when, among other things, it is either rising or culminating, and also to a lesser extent when setting or crossing the lower meridian at the locality of birth. These four areas of the astrologer's circular diurnal chart, corresponding to the Ascendant, MC, Descendant and IC respectively (see Chapter 2, page 24), have been found to be more frequently occupied by certain planets in the charts of eminent professionals than chance would normally allow. For instance, if you take a sample of eminent sportspeople, the planet Mars is found to be statistically more prominent in their charts than in those of a control group of more sedentary men and women. To a lesser extent it was found that the planet Jupiter shows up strongly in the charts of eminent politicians and executives; the planet Saturn in the charts of scientists and physicians; and the Moon in the charts of successful writers and creative people. All this is in tune with the traditional astrological correlations applying to these bodies. And although Gauquelin's pioneering studies still have their critics, his work has been successfully replicated.

'Gauquelin also extended his work to heredity, examining the charts of parents and children. In a survey covering one hundred thousand births, he discovered that if a particular planet is strong in the chart of a parent, or both parents, then it is statistically more likely to be so in the chart of the child. In other words, if your father had a prominent Saturn in his nativity, it is quite likely that you do as well, and therefore that your children will. This also appears even more likely during times of increased geomagnetic activity – generated, as we have seen, by the solar wind acting upon the upper atmosphere of the Earth. Interestingly, only in cases of natural childbirth does this planetary relationship exist. If the births are artificially manipulated the relationship breaks down.[62]

'There have been numerous further statistical experiments relating to astrology during the past few years, in fact a great many indeed, as a glance at the on-line data-base of the Research Group for the Critical Study of Astrology will reveal.[63] And although the subject of astrology has never lent itself at all well to the reductionist approach of statistical analysis, and although studies of this kind certainly do have their detractors, the results are, nonetheless, encouraging. The influence that you spoke of does exist, and this has been amply demonstrated. Moreover, the planets are far from being the quiet, passive objects you seem to imagine them to be. Often bodies, such as Jupiter, which emit powerful radio waves, have jumps in their rates of emission, which exceed those of the Sun. These are also related to detectable storms, but in planetary atmospheres, not solar.[64]

'As we have already seen, the magnetosphere of the Earth is highly sensitive to variations in radiation from space, solar or otherwise. This Earth-field extends at least twenty times the distance of our planet to the Sun and becomes, therefore, one vast receiver of solar, planetary and galactic emissions. All the planets, and our own Moon too, have similar fields, all intermingling. And due to the resonance effect, the vast distances you earlier spoke of are now no longer significant in terms of the solar system, an organism whose parts are so closely integrated that it is no longer possible to think of them as discrete entities at all.

'All this is persuasive enough, but we can also look even further afield for possible sources of influence. In this context, the work of the Italian chemist, Giorgio Piccardi, is definitely worth mentioning as it seems to imply a galactic force field acting upon the Earth. Piccardi was puzzled by the seemingly random variations in chemical reactions that take place during most chemical experiments. Previously, scientists thought these to be due to chance alone. By placing a copper screen over his experiments, however, which consisted of measuring the rate of precipitation of chemicals from water at body temperature, Piccardi discovered that these variations disappeared. The disturbing agent, he concluded, came from space. Many years of research located these sources in the Sun, Moon and planets – as might be expected. Equally important, however, was a further strong background variation that fluctuated regularly according to the time of year. This was ultimately traced to the movement of the Earth within the galactic field itself, a kind of corkscrew motion produced from the Earth's annual orbit around the Sun combining with the Sun's own motion within the galaxy. In the month of March (the time of the spring equinox and the start of the astrologer's zodiac, by the way), the Earth's movement meets the galactic field head-on, while during September its motion runs counter to the field of force.[65] The relevance of the zodiac to this is, indeed, significant, since the tropical zodiac itself is essentially a direct function of the Earth's orbit about the Sun.

'Now, the liquids which Piccardi used in these experiments are technically termed aqueous colloidal systems, and they are ones on which most life-processes are based. The reactions, moreover, are at their most sensitive at temperatures of thirty-four to forty degrees centigrade – in other words that of warm-blooded animals including ourselves. Like the admittedly far more simple experiments of Kollerstrom and his predecessors, these responses are significant in terms of the maintenance of organic life, indicating a definite correlation with external cosmic stimuli. Piccardi himself, though not in any sense an astrologer, was quick to stress this point.

'Yet for all that this is true, and for all the irrefutable scientific evidence that astrology now has at its disposal, it is also a fact that astrologers themselves frequently remain unimpressed by research or experimental evidence, mainly owing to the fact that influence, as such, is not a necessary component of their art. Astrology can get along quite nicely without influence, and always has done. The idea of synchronised events, of correspondences in nature between the macro and microcosm, are sufficient to explain why astrology works. Synchronicity, thus named by the psychologist Carl Jung, has as its basis the notion that every moment of time has a certain quality that is manifest in any number of other possibly quite unrelated phenomena.[66]

'A good example of synchronicity is in popular music. An old number is played on the radio, a song you suddenly remember from years back. You immediately recall lots of other things: where you spent your holidays that summer, the fashions and clothes people were wearing, who was prime minister, or president, at the time, what wars were being waged, and so on. Somehow the old record sums up all these totally unrelated things. Not only is it a focus for memories but also it seems to be a product of the entire world as it was at just that particular moment. And indeed how could it be anything else?

'Time stamps its mark on events; one event shares in every other. It is this special quality of time and place that can be related to the movements of natural bodies, be it the migration of birds in winter or the aspects of the Moon and Saturn in an astrological chart. These are all pointers, indicators of parallel events, but they don't need to be connected to these events by any direct causal relationship whatsoever. So astrology, being a mathematically accurate record and projection of movements in the sky, becomes an ideal indicator of the quality of each moment of time. Once this concept is grasped, not only does astrology make sense but so too does much of life itself. This is perhaps the greatest contribution that astrology has to make to our understanding of nature and the human consciousness.

'As far as influence is concerned, therefore, yes it does seem to exist but it also functions deep within the framework of synchronised events. A good illustration of this can be found if we return to the research into human experiences here on Earth, and electrical disturbances in the atmosphere. You can say that these are actually caused by disturbances in the Sun's photosphere but these, in turn, could be related to the movements of planets and the angular momentum of all the other bodies in the solar system, including the Earth, which is where we came in.

'The connections are endless. Cause and effect, as such, is a concept disappearing from both astrology and science.

147

Everything influences everything else; not least of all the observer.[67] Astrology is certainly very much a part of this observational process. And if it also deals with real demonstrable influences – as I hope you now realise it does – then, like the eye, it colours and changes that which it observes. Like the eye, it creates a wonderful picture, based on form and reality but with the worthy addition of human understanding and meaning. It is this creative dimension, producing order and beauty out of the data of blind chaos, which astrologers prize above all else and is why simplistic talk of cause and effect, influences from a distance, and statistical studies are, ultimately, of little real concern to those who practise and interpret the world in this way.'

Note: Although you can probably come up with endless examples of subtle influences and force fields, a confirmed sceptic might still hit back with arguments based on sceptical research into astrological practice. We will have a little more to say about research and statistical studies later on in Chapter 12. But for now, it is worth being aware that one of the most compelling (to the sceptics) pieces of evidence against the validity of astrology is those oft-repeated 'experiments' in which astrological readings are switched and those volunteers who provided their birth data are given back, without their knowledge, readings that do not belong to them. Although these readings are fabricated and do not relate to the birth data of the subjects themselves they are nonetheless frequently met with approval and accepted by the volunteers as being 'highly accurate', 'insightful' and so on. This, according to the sceptics, is irrefutable proof that astrology is without validity and cannot possibly have any effect on people's lives. Your reply need not be lengthy:

Combat: 'What you are referring to seems to demonstrate what we already know: that people can be easily tricked. It shows that people taking part in experiments do so usually in a spirit of openness and trust, which is a credit to them. But, as every con-artist knows, it is not too difficult to mislead people under such circumstances. These are actually experiments in human nature, not astrology. They do not indicate that astrology is wrong, moreover – no more than, say, presenting a misleading property survey to an eager house-buyer renders the science of surveying wrong. Nor do these experiments indicate that astrologers are disingenuous – only that the designers of the experiments are.'

Critique 12: Relevance

'All right, so I am willing to believe there could be some rational and even scientific basis to astrology. But really, what use is it all? We live in a world of fast-moving, hard-hitting practicalities. People are sharp and cynical: they're no longer concerned with ideas like this. Even orthodox religion has to struggle to be heard. People expect results, tangible proof and practical application of knowledge.

'Not only this, but to be of any real use at all, astrology would have to impinge so dangerously on individual human rights as to be unworkable. You can't direct people when and where to have children, or when to do this or do that. Everyone needs to make their own decisions, not to live in some sinister theocracy under the dictates of an astrological priesthood. The whole notion of taking astrology seriously is not only fundamentally distasteful but also, in social or political terms, downright dangerous.

'Even if you were to direct the private lives of individuals like this, the real practical relevance of the exercise would be negligible compared to the vastly stronger external forces of, say, economics, politics, social movements or climate change. Astrology may be true; it is certainly an attractive and neat proposition, elegant and delightful in its own way; but really what use is it to anyone?'

Combat: 'Certainly no astrologer I know would want to be party to any regime that orders people about or tells them how to behave. Astrologers do not wish to become priests, as you put it; they just want to continue helping others and to earn their living doing something both useful and enjoyable. Moreover, there are plenty of practical uses for astrology other than regulating birth times in some sort of futuristic utopian society. Here, for example, are just some of the many practical applications of astrology, in all its many and diverse forms.

'Firstly, a study of astrology is essential for a proper understanding of history. It is impossible to understand the present or speculate on the future without some knowledge of the past. Even if you start from the dubious premise that astrology is intrinsically worthless, you will at least need to acknowledge the enormous extent to which astrological doctrine has permeated and often directly influenced each and every period of history – at least through to the age of the Enlightenment. We cannot possibly pretend to understand the Greeks, the Elizabethans – anybody at all – without considering the one continually popular belief system practised at varying levels of sophistication by all classes of society and at all times: astrology. Without it the historian lacks one of the great master keys to truly sympathetic understanding of the minds and feelings of those that have gone before. The study of astrology in this context is recognised today as a legitimate academic activity – as demonstrated by degree courses in Cultural Astronomy and Astrology now offered by certain universities and colleges.[68] In the UK this is led by the Sophia Project, the aim of which is to advance the study of astrology and cultural astronomy in British institutions of higher education, recognising that there are, indeed, many areas of academic interest where the subject is applicable.

'In a practical sense, today's astrology is best used for helping individual people to control their own futures through self-understanding and perhaps some degree of fore-knowledge and anticipation. This is natal astrology at its best, and is currently the area in which astrological principles are the most extensively employed. Here it is possible to make such a highly positive contribution to personal well-being and understanding, that society as a whole can only benefit as a consequence. In this context, the importance of the birth chart cannot be underestimated because, it could be argued, our future is determined only to a minimum extent by what happens to us, the rest is determined by how we react to it. This is why astrologers, even if they are not interested in forecasting, believe that character, itself, is destiny. A person's chart can tell us about how an individual thinks and perceives the world. Thoughts lead to actions, and actions become habits. Habits, in turn, shape the personality and how we are perceived by others, and this ultimately determines our range of opportunities – in other words our future and, if you like, our luck as well.

'Because of this, working psychologists will now occasionally avail themselves of astrological analyses on behalf of their clients, especially if family or case histories are not available. The birth chart with its unique insight into the character and emotional background of the patient, is probably about as near anyone will ever get to being able to look at a map of the psyche. Not that any self-respecting psychologist would base his entire approach on astrology; that would be foolish. But it is one more string to the bow, and increasingly recognised as such by astute practitioners. Astrology can blend easily with most counselling techniques, and therein lies its value for the specialist.[69]

'It is when it comes to serving the community at large, however, that astrology can really come into its own. The branch of astrology dealing with compatibility and relationships, called synastry, has as great a potential for counselling in areas like social work or marriage guidance as it has for private individuals. In the East, many families still consult an astrologer for matrimonial matters, compatibility and timing. In all cases, partners can discover something valuable about the possible unfolding of the other's personality over the years. Many broken homes can be helped to rebuild, and all the suffering associated with separation of children from parents, together with the ultimately damaging effect this has on society, could be greatly ameliorated through a reasonable and balanced use of the synastry technique both prior to and during any relationship.

'Synastry doesn't need to stop there, though. It can extend beyond purely personal relationships into groups and organisations, and has enormous potential in industry, sports and education. For example, a teacher with access to the birth data of a difficult pupil would be able to receive valuable information concerning the possible root of the problem – the pupil's problem and maybe the teacher's in terms of relating to that particular individual. Synastry can act as a clearing house for those wishing to organise working groups, teams, parties, events and study-projects of all kinds. This is because it is able to compare any number of different charts, and produce guidelines for group compatibility and timing.

'To return to the individual approach, perhaps the most obvious use of astrology lies in the field of medicine. The two subjects once went hand in hand, and still do in most Eastern branches of healing. In this country alternative local practitioners in many ethnic communities make use of rudimentary astrology, and much of this could be of advantage to orthodox doctors in search of an additional dimension of sympathetic understanding, and who are also aware of the ever-growing popular conviction that in clinical practice the whole person and not merely the symptoms need to be treated.[70] Knowing the psychology of each patient is every bit as important as the physiology. Here in the West, astrological data can equally well be applied by those working in the fields of alternative or complementary medicine as a means of confirming diagnoses, just as it always has been elsewhere in other parts of the world.

'In addition, there are also less well publicised uses of astrology, in particular economic forecasting and stock market prediction. This is not to be confused with those publicity-seeking expert astrologers who often make their findings and predictions public, and who are frequently wrong. Behind the scenes, many a powerful investor will use astrology together with the usual considerations of fundamental and technical market analysis to plan investment decisions. This is because the major financial markets of the world are often swayed by totally psychological conditions and moods. Astrology provides a useful key to understanding these moods, although it has to be remembered that this will always remain a highly specialised subject.[71]

'The branch of astrology known as horary, the judgement of events and specific questions was widespread in former times, and has almost unlimited uses in day-to-day affairs even now. Human nature and aspirations do not change, and nor do the questions that most people need to have answers to. Love and partnerships are centre-stage as always. Lost or stolen articles still need to be recovered. The future course of a business or a relationship still needs to be determined. In horary, questions concerning practically any subject at all can be approached by erecting a chart for the moment the question itself is raised or first comes to light. Subsequent examination of all the many variables present in the chart can then usually provide an answer, or at least some valuable guidance on how to move forward with the problem. And if you think that using astrology to assist in crime detection sounds pie in the sky, let me assure you that horary was used for precisely that purpose in the days before any organised police force existed. Eminently practical, horary astrology was perhaps at its height during the fifteenth and sixteenth centuries, but is enjoying something of a revival in recent times and has many well-documented successes to its credit.[72] Great experience is needed for this kind of work, however, and it is again a very specialised subject – though no less relevant and useful, for all that.

'A more widespread knowledge of astrology can bring greater tolerance and patience into the everyday world. To comprehend the other person's point of view, to be able to find a key to those moods which can sweep over us all at times: astrology can help everyone develop such sympathies and abilities. For it is firstly within the substantial world of reality that astrology functions, and here that everyone may learn to know themselves, their strengths and weaknesses, their previous history and perhaps a little of their life's purpose as well. Through self-knowledge and unity, it can guide and inspire in a wholly practical way, providing information on periods of life when advance or retreat, confidence or modesty, can best be put to use. Favourable times for action; warnings of impulsive tendencies; unconscious promptings, and possible sources of mental or physical imbalance: all these can be revealed and adjusted through correct astrological analysis. None of this encroaches one bit on individual free will or choice. Quite the contrary.

'It is wrong, therefore, to say that astrology is irrelevant or somehow out of tune with the modern way of life. People are keener than ever now to investigate the world of the unseen. There is also a ever-present need in most people to be inspired at times, a desire to be re-assured that there is more to this world than the daily grind of modern life – behaving like some poor desperate rodent trapped on a treadmill each day, and grinding themselves into the ground with continuous greed, envy and resignation. This is not what being human is all about. Astrology can lift the mind and the spirit above that kind of dark, banal world and provide a light to those in need.

'It can be abused, of course. Any belief system can become a political tool. And any skill can be employed in a misguided way. With astrology, however, this has rarely been the case, and the more aware the general public becomes of its genuine scope and content, the less likely the unwelcome, controlling kind of scenario you mentioned earlier becomes. In one form or another astrology has always existed, and been of use and there is no reason to doubt that this process will continue. In this, it does not seek to rule people or to eliminate mistakes, nor could it possibly ever hope to do so, since mistakes are an essential ingredient of progress and learning. But it can, and does, when asked, offer guidance in times of doubt or crisis. It can and does, when asked, offer assurance and inspiration in times of progress and stability.'

So ends our reply to our final critique, and so ends also Part Two of this book. The relevance of astrology, however, is something we will certainly keep in mind as we continue into Part Three. Here we will be looking at just where astrology stands at the present time, its status in the community at large, where it is heading and what all this could mean for you and me.

Where is Astrology Going?

CHAPTER 9

The Arm of the Law, The Hounds of the Press

It would be wonderful if the profession of astrology could move on into the twenty-first century free of ambiguity and the taint of superstition. Yet the same problems that Ptolemy complained of in the second century still bedevil the subject today: the impostors, the charlatans, the quack astrologers, along with the gullible members of the public who give them credence.

The tragedy facing the respectable astrologer today is the tendency to be tarred with the same brush as the peddler of cheap internet sites or sun-sign journalism. This confusion is nothing new. It has always been equally prevalent in appraising the role of astrology in historical terms. An historian will discover how a certain distinguished writer of antiquity disapproved of 'the Chaldeans and their superstitious beliefs' and assume this to be an attack against astrology. This is because many a Chaldean immigrant in classical times practised number-divination and gave this a veneer of respectability by calling it astrological. The word Chaldean, therefore, came to be synonymous with astrology and superstition alike. A curious quirk of history, this: a little like saying that because there are nudists living in Scotland that all Scotsmen are nudists. As a consequence of this kind of generalisation, astrology today seems to remain largely outside of the usual regulations and trading standards demanded of the rest of the business community, while in some circles it is possibly even assumed that anybody who dabbles in such things and is subsequently cheated or let down probably deserves all that is coming to them. Self-regulation from within the major astrological bodies is, however, already addressing this problem and organisations like the Faculty of Astrological Studies or the Association of Professional Astrologers in the UK are increasingly active in fostering ever-higher standards of professionalism among their members.

This development is to be welcomed, because the legal position of astrology and its practitioners has always been ambiguous, if not also occasionally precarious. And in a sense, what was true in the days of the witch trials in the seventeenth century is still true today: the subject tends to be lumped together with magic and the occult. Many who have attempted to teach or talk on astrology locally will be painfully aware of this confusion. Advertisements can be banned, lectures or after-dinner speeches scrapped – all by public outcry from disgruntled individuals who seem to emerge from the woodwork on such occasions and who, by their sheer oddness, make astrologers look quite staid and humdrum by comparison.

This lack of clarity between the sober, respectable practice of astrology and the sensational dark aspects of the occult is, however, understandable when we look at the history of astrology in Europe. In the past, often the best astrologers tended to dabble in the occult, in alchemy, the evocation of spirit, and so on. A figure who personifies this tendency is the great sixteenth-century astrologer and scientist Dr John Dee. Dee was a man of many talents and occupations: a typical Renaissance man who mixed as easily within the worlds of espionage and diplomacy as he did in those of navigation and engineering. His vision and imagination were legendary at the court of Elizabeth I, but his skills, often incomprehensible to the majority of people, aroused accusations of witchcraft. On one occasion, while Dee was out of the country, his house and library – in many ways the forerunner of the British Library, containing many priceless books of antiquity – was burned to the ground by an angry mob, on the popular assumption that he was a wicked sorcerer and conjuror of spirits. Dee did, however, certainly possess a lively interest in occult subjects, and perhaps the unease felt by his contemporaries was real enough.

It is perhaps fruitless to speculate on the reasons why such brilliant individuals occupied themselves to such an extent with magic and what seems to modern people as irrational fixations. I do not believe it is possible to understand so easily the minds of those who lived so long ago, nor am I wholly convinced that 'irrational' is a fair description of what is clearly the precursor of much of our current day psychology and psychoanalysis. If we tend at times to imbue historical characters with our own thoughts, awarding them our own particular vices, fears and pompositics, and then judge them according to our own knowledge and standards, it can only take us further from not closer to comprehension. As an astrologer or as an enthusiast of the subject, you might not enjoy being confused with magicians and fortune tellers, with ghost hunters and spiritualists, but, like it or not, it is all part of the legacy left to us by men such as Dee, Cardan, Nostradamus, Ficino and Crowley, as well as many lesser luminaries, and to the hostility of the Church to much of their work.

This last point is important, for the Church represented the establishment during the medieval period and the Renaissance – a position of such prominence that it is little wonder that its occasional outbreak of censure has percolated down to the present day, a censure that has been reflected and enshrined in many of the laws and acts of parliament that have been passed since Dee's times, and in the rather quaint terminology these often employ, with mention of itinerant astrologers, rogues and vagabonds, etc.

Although in the UK the earlier Witchcraft Act of 1735 was repealed by a less damning Fraudulent Mediums Act in 1951, astrologers at this time were still classed along with crystal gazers and spiritualists. Moreover, the apparently antisocial nature of astrologers' work has even led them to be included in the Vagrancy Acts of 1824 and 1829! Remarkable as it may seem, much of this legislation still holds relevance for astrologers today, although naturally there is no recent history of anyone being tried for witchcraft. (Homeless or itinerant astrologers are, thankfully, also a comparative rarity.)

In the light of this, the whole legal question may seem rather academic. However, astrologers themselves should never under any circumstances be complacent. Any kind of fraudulent practice is against the law, of course. And anyone, astrologer or otherwise, who offers something for sale when unable or unwilling to deliver what they promise is in danger of transgressing not only the Fraudulent Mediums Act but also, perhaps more seriously, the Trades Descriptions Laws of their own country – which can impose heavy penalties on anyone who deceives the public by making false claims for their goods or services. In Europe, measures to protect the consumer are always being strengthened and will doubtless become more and more supportive of conventional trade and commerce at the expense of alternative life-style choices such as complementary medicine and spiritual exploration.

It is vital, therefore, to understand the essentially open and provisional nature of astrological interpretation. Predictive work should never be couched in the language of finality and hard-and-fast forecasts. It is certainly always a danger, not only to the astrologer but also to the client, to give the impression that one's luck or fortune will suddenly change overnight simply by parting with a little cash and slavishly following the dictates of a telephone reading, an e-mail or computer-generated analysis. Yet this is precisely the message many of the more down-market astrologers who advertise in magazines or on the internet brazenly give to their readers via quotes from their customers. 'Since writing to you my life has been transformed dramatically,' says Mrs B. from Manchester. 'I can't believe the change in my luck!' says Mr D. from London SW1.

Special care is always taken by serious astrologers as to what is said and written in the course of their work and in their promotional literature. The laws of slander and libel apply as much to astrologers as to anyone else. This becomes particularly important when a third party is involved: for example, in the case where a client may have requested a natal analysis of his or her unscrupulous boss, or where a woman has asked for a chart comparison with her unfaithful husband. The dangers of character defamation in such cases are obvious, especially as the astrologer often unwittingly takes the side of the client. A balanced mixture of honesty and diplomacy is essential at all times. Sympathy, meanwhile – and though laudable – is not a duty.

It is hoped that in the future more and more astrologers will be trained professionally by schools that offer internationally recognised qualifications, and that they will in turn become well-versed in the methodology of presenting information. Indeed, as a good common-sense guide, most astrologers in practice today could certainly do a lot worse than follow the code of ethics as presented by some of these bodies (see Figure 5, page 49). The Faculty of Astrological Studies, the Mayo School and their counterparts in other countries, try to instil a sense of moderation in their students, and stress the need for transmitting this through to the public. In fact, the pathway towards a professional diploma from these bodies is one that any astrologer, budding or already in practice, would do well to pursue, even if he or she feels this may not be absolutely essential to their career in material terms. Established in 1948, the Faculty has enormous practical experience in the profession, and the open days and seminars that it stages regularly attract the best speakers in the field.

Some astrologers, especially full-time professionals, will of course have their own insurance cover against legal expenses or liabilities. In the UK, the Association of Professional Astrologers likewise works under a strict code of ethics and has insurance cover for its members as well – who are all qualified to practise to the highest standards. In some parts of the world, however, and perhaps where such umbrella organisations are not always available, astrologers will go as far as to ask their clients to sign a disclaimer prior to undertaking written work. This, in theory at least, absolves the astrologer from responsibility should his or advice or predictions prove in some sense damaging to the client. Something along the following lines ...

'I understand you make no claim to any special or occult power ... I understand that I am not asking you to tell my fortune in any sense, nor do I understand that you attempt or pretend to do so.'

Note that the disclaimer from which this was taken was at the time being used by a consultant astrologer. If you are in practice and you wish to design your own, you may be wise to seek legal advice on the exact wording and the degree to which it is binding in law – though whether such an approach is really satisfactory is perhaps a matter of taste. It certainly cannot be particularly inspiring for a client to receive a document of this kind. Moreover, a correctly worded analysis should normally obviate the need for such cumbersome arrangements.

Media Games

Of equal importance to maintaining personal integrity is the matter of the astrologer's exposure to the press and to TV journalism. With regard to matters of public reputation, astrologers need to take special care they do not run foul of the

161

media. I am thinking particularly of the kind of 'Sex, Drugs and the Vicar' kind of coverage that is often found in the Sunday papers or the local news bulletins. Journalists are keen on sniffing out scandal, and the 'occult' – an area into which they usually insist on placing astrology – has always been a favourite quarry.

This is perhaps the greatest paradox, that despite the media's penchant for Sun-sign journalism and even, it should be noted, in giving their newspapers strong-selling astro-names like

The Sun, The Star, The Mercury or *The Globe,* they still retain an inherent dislike for any of those strange individuals audacious enough to take the subject seriously. This tendency to take away with one hand what is given with the other is, however, wholly typical of the profession. A newspaper that will gleefully print provocative pin-ups and pro-macho sex surveys on one page, will indignantly report a story of prostitution or rape on the next, all without the slightest vestige of unease over their possible hypocrisy.

Television can appear fairer, and may often seem to be informative on subjects like astrology. But there are vested interests and world views to be protected here as well, laws and codes that must be adhered to and which are, at bottom pro-materialistic, atheistic and essentially anti-astrology. Nowhere has this hostility been more obvious that in the recent proposal for changes in 2003 to the programming code of the ITC, the UK's television regulator (now called OFCOM). Guidelines for broadcasters intending to show astrology on television included the following injunction:

'Demonstrations of predictive practices, whether "psychic" or otherwise (e.g. horoscopes, palmistry), are acceptable only when they are presented as entertainment or are the subject of legitimate investigation. They should not include specific advice to particular contributors or viewers about health or medical matters or about personal finance. They should not be included at times when large numbers of children are expected to be watching.'[1]

So it is perfectly OK to have us all watching people arguing, fighting and killing each other every five minutes on our screens, but not to expose our younger citizens to the dangers of learning about astrology! When one realises that the multinational corporations controlling the present world-order (and which seek to manipulate our lives from the cradle to the grave) have only just managed to shake off the inconvenience of religion in many parts the world, it is hardly any wonder that they should resist any tendency for people to use their minds for metaphysical exploration through the vehicle of something like astrology. No wonder, too, that most programs on TV concerning astrology are so toe-curlingly embarrassing. They have to be dressed up as entertainment! The message of the ITC was clear – don't get into any intelligent discussion about astrology. People might start to take it seriously.

In this respect, nothing much has changed. The ITC's clause of 'legitimate investigation' notwithstanding, even if we go back as far as 1975 to preparations for the BBC's science review programme Horizon and its investigation of astrology we see the hand of political caution firmly raised. Although the programme itself when screened had the appearance of impartiality, much positive experimental work was excluded from the final presentation. The metal salt experiments of Kollerstrom (see page 143) were filmed, but despite the fact that they showed irrefutable evidence for a planetary effect (or perhaps precisely *because* they showed irrefutable evidence for a planetary effect) this particular contribution was dropped, and the footage itself destroyed![2] Yes, destroyed. Not even an impartial researcher in the near or distant future will be able to trace this highly interesting experiment in the film archives of the BBC.

In the same way as most television companies rely on advertising revenue from multinational companies intent on perpetuating the consumer society at every possible opportunity, so too do newspapers and their proprietors. This is because the price you pay for the newspaper barely covers the cost of distribution. Advertising is everything to them in terms of revenue, and so it should not come as any great surprise that this can affect the slant of the journalism therein. In addition to this, some papers also like to present themselves as being custodians of good taste or of wishing to maintain scientific and academic standards. This is a heady mixture that almost invites the occasional crusade of self-righteousness to take centre stage. Add the odd disgruntled scientist or two into the mix and the results can be unfortunate to say the least.

Take, for example, the instance in 2003 when a major Sunday broadsheet in the UK printed a paper co-authored by one of astrology's most clever and persistent critics, Geoffrey Dean. The original paper was, apparently, published some time previously in the *Journal of Consciousness Studies* but was taken up by the newspaper and heralded as fresh evidence that astrology is an invalid belief system when put to the test – and other somewhat less flattering statements. Having a bash at astrology again! Oh well. It didn't exactly have the astrological community quaking in its boots, but did arouse a fair bit of smug 'See I told you so' statements from the unbelievers on the one hand and quite a lot of angry reactions from the more militant believers on the other.[3]

The article itself, though worthy enough, is not easy reading, especially if you do not possess qualifications in statistical research or enormous patience, but was – according to its critics anyway – apparently a collection of rather dated experiments and statistical re-evaluations of experiments conducted by astrologers themselves. Mr Dean is very fond of and, it must be said, often very successful at debunking experiments that have endeavoured in the past to provide some proof of astrology. The fact that the debunking itself is sometimes seen to be wanting does not appear to discourage the detractors – and actually it would be rather disappointing if it ever did. Astrology, like everything else, needs its critics. And if the campaign is conducted on an intelligent and rational basis, so much the better. We can handle it.

What sometimes happens, unfortunately, is that when an editor or journalist with a particular axe to grind gets hold of work of this kind and subsequently attempts to convince their readership that some kind of amazing revelation has just occurred that renders astrology meaningless for all eternity, then a lot of people can become misled, and a lot of hot air and animosity is generated that usually does little credit to all concerned. One of the least attractive features of this episode was that – presumably in the interests of 'fair play' – the paper contacted some prominent astrologers a few days prior to publication, inviting comment on what was to be a very lengthy article attacking their profession, but copies of which they were unfortunately unable to provide at the time! I suppose that's a bit like phoning up somebody in the middle of the night and asking, 'What do you think of my new three-piece suit?' without them ever having seen it. We need not give this dismal incident any further consideration here, but it is sadly illustrative of what does take place every once in a while.

On a more encouraging note, both TV and newspapers alike now often feature that slightly more positive and responsible style of investigative journalism that acts as watchdog to the consumer – though this, unfortunately, can often be unpleasantly suspicious of anyone connected with psychology, the healing or counselling arts, and sometimes takes the form of setting traps for certain practitioners to fall into. So do tread carefully in this area – especially when asked to participate in 'experiments' by seemingly friendly and innocuous journalists (or people posing as them) who already have a secret agenda and who want to enlist you for experiments already primed to fail, either through naivety or simple deviousness. For instance, much of the body of critical study ranged against astrology uses the ploy of attributing something to the subject which it does not inherently possess and then demonstrating that the *something* in question does not work – and that therefore (according to their own strange kind of logic) that astrology doesn't work either.

A good example of this would be to state that astrology relies on clairvoyance, and then set up an experiment to show that astrologers do not perform very well at clairvoyance. So astrology is shown to be wrong. Naturally, astrologers do not usually avail themselves of clairvoyance at all. Instead, they use precise birth data and then carefully calculate and painstakingly analyse the resulting charts using specific rules and procedures handed down over the centuries. For the zealous detractors of astrology, however, this is of no interest. They have done their experiment, got their story and the astrologers have been shown to be wanting in credibility. They are not clairvoyant after all.

One really has to wonder what exactly could be the motivation behind such exercises, or the perpetrators of them. They are usually highly qualified academics, basking in the sunlight of scientific respectability and yet who for one reason or another simply cannot resist kicking sand in the faces of the little guys on the beach. And it gets worse. Even more extreme instances have occurred in the past, engineered with all the usual finesse of the bully, which also illustrate the desperation that many of astrology's critics must feel at times. Here, for example, a sceptical journalist masquerading as a potential client approaches an astrologer for career advice, but instead of supplying him with his own genuine birth data, presents him with that of, say, an infamous murderer. Not surprisingly, the astrologer tries to make the best of it all in good faith and, with the right kind of prompting and clever questioning from the investigator, will make pronouncements to the effect that the person concerned would be suitable for working with others and helping their community and so on. How clever! And it does make a good story

But wait! Is this sort of thing an experiment in astrology or an experiment in deviousness? You decide. Again, this is an example of somebody attributing to astrology a quality which it does not profess to have – in this case some special kind of talent for spotting murderers. Most astrologers are quite clear on the fact that the charts of unpleasant people are often very similar to those of good people. Similarly, a king's chart can be identical to a pauper's, and a saint's to a sinner's. This is because a good person, possessed of reasonable moral character will always make the best of a bad astrological make-up, while the bad person will generally succeed in making the worst of it. Given knowledge of these basic facts – that is, knowing who one is dealing with – the astrologer can then use the chart to draw some intelligent conclusions. But that wouldn't give journalists the headline they need, or sceptics the ammunition they long for.

One also wonders whether those who so fervently try to debunk astrology in this way would do the same with other professions. When they visit their local doctor and he asks 'What seems to be the matter?' do they reply with something like, 'Well, you're the doctor, you tell me!' – and then present him with several separate lists of symptoms, mostly belonging to other people, before demanding that he pick out the correct one and make a diagnosis? Equally absurd. Yet studies of this kind are continually being foisted on astrologers and subsequently proclaimed by their creators as 'proof' that astrology does not work.

For all that these shabby little episodes are undoubtedly going to continue, the investigative eye of the media, and of the sceptic is still probably, on balance, a positive aid for astrology as a whole. Mainstream journalism, of which the above example is certainly not representative, can help to weed out the tricksters, the plainly fraudulent and bad astrologers, who are thankfully few in number perhaps precisely because of this kind of vigilance. And for every science correspondent and every editor with a grudge against the mystical dimension to life, there are plenty who are open-minded and fair. Sometimes they have even been known to defend astrology! As is so often the case, the freedom of the press – despite its occasional foray into the astrology-bashing arena – turns out to be one of the most valuable assets of any free society, and we should, all of us, be big enough and wise enough not to wish it ill.

Astrologers in the future need not go in fear, therefore. If they are sincere they will be spared. What they have to do, though, is foster awareness: a continued familiarity with the real world and the ever-changing climate of public opinion. For it is amazing how little cause most people need to feel indignant and hard done by, and suddenly to demand an exposé of the culprit. Astrologers need to be mindful of sensitive issues, therefore, and monitor within themselves any fault or indiscretion that might encourage the attentions of crusading journalists. Like any profession, astrology will only ever be as good as its practitioners. And again, as has been mentioned so often in these pages, modesty, humility and a firm reluctance to promise miraculous predictions and revelations, be it to fee-paying clients or to your friends and acquaintances, remain the best defence of all. None of this is easy of course. There are many obstacles, and many of them unwittingly set by astrologers themselves. There are cautionary tales that need to be heeded. Let's look at some of these next.

CHAPTER 10

Cautionary Tales

Since nature has on the whole not been able to make us perfect, it is only fair that she has at least made us blind to our faults. Were this the only reason, it would be sufficient for us to be cautious, to step back occasionally and check our own behaviour. As an enthusiast or practitioner of astrology, you are first and foremost a guardian of a venerable and precious tradition, and you must conduct your affairs accordingly, that is – as far as possible – impeccably.

> 'The Sage keeps the One and becomes the standard for the world.
> He does not display himself; therefore he shines.
> He does not approve himself; therefore he is noted.
> He does not praise himself; therefore he has merit.
> He does not glory in himself; therefore he excels.
> And because he does not compete; therefore no one in the world can compete with him.'[1]

Inspired by these wise words, the rest of this chapter deals with some of the major *do's* and *don'ts* of astrological practice: seven special cautionary tales that anyone involved with this venerable and controversial subject would do well to heed.

The Specialist's Tale

First of all let's have the story of the astrologer, usually a highly paid professional, who although an excellent practitioner may lack any real knowledge of the wider implications of his or her art – or simply of what is taking place in the real world – the relation of astrology to the sciences, to history, to psychology and social affairs, and so on. This person is often left at a disadvantage when confronted by experts in any of these fields, or might also be too deeply immersed in his or her own ways to be of any real use or assistance to those who come for help or guidance.

Continuing Professional Development (that is, keeping up to speed on all the latest developments in one's sphere of work) is a concept now entering many professions, such as medicine and

teaching – and astrology should not be aloof from this occasional moment of self-appraisal, either. Every astrologer needs to remain approachable: not to become walled in by specialisation. This is going to become more and more important during the years ahead, as the world moves further and further into a situation where knowledge has to become more compartmentalised. Then, as never before, we will need people who can see the whole picture, contemplate alternatives. An astrologer who can provide this service will always be invaluable to his or her clients, especially in times of crises when it often seems there is no way out, nowhere to turn. On the other hand, the narrow, specialist astrologer – perhaps busy on some unique nugget of vital research, or suddenly excited and deeply involved in some rare and arcane corner of astrology's past – can simply lose touch with reality or else becomes caught in the same predicament as those they seek to advise: unable to see the wood for the trees. Everyone suffers as a consequence.

170

Moreover, when a client asks for an astrological analysis they are probably expecting something fairly main-stream and not too specialised or esoteric from their astrologer. They will probably be expecting it in plain English as well. As an astrologer you should be mindful of this and keep both feet firmly on the ground when communicating your findings – mindful, too, that astrology does not have all the answers. There are other things in life to be put into the equation when judging the character of another human being. Their health, their environment, their parenting, their schooling – these are just as important, and just as influential as any piece of astrology, and must be included in your judgement and, if applicable, any forecasting you may be engaged in on their behalf.

It is vital to keep an open mind, therefore, to keep learning – to read, listen and to study anything and everything that seems in any way relevant to astrology. And most things are relevant. Astrology embraces all of life, from the sacred to the profane.

The Prima Donna's Tale

The 'persona' is a term employed by psychology to describe our self-image, the face or mask we all, to a greater or lesser extent, put on each day in order to fulfil our social functions. The traffic warden becomes wholly a traffic warden the moment he or she dons the uniform and takes to the streets, otherwise we might not take him or her quite so seriously as we do. When challenged, we often defend our persona vehemently, as if our lives depended on it. This can result in a genuine neurosis in certain individuals, who may identify with the persona to such a degree that they lose touch with the real inner self and its needs. Some of those most vehement critics of astrology and of all things mystical tend to fall into this trap. These individuals are, by and large, a fairly decent and intelligent bunch but when they feel their life-purpose and beliefs are being usurped by lesser beings like astrologers, they become very upset indeed. The persona is threatened.

A great danger for the astrologer, too, is that of taking his or her persona so seriously as to be beyond reach. These distant, formal figures of mystery are not likely to be able to serve the public nor to inspire much trust in even those closest to them. Also, enthusiasts of astrology who, even if ever so sincere, appear

R.S.P

exceptionally eccentric to the vast majority of people, are not likely to advance their cause, no matter how well informed or erudite they might be. This is perhaps a rather sad state of affairs; for the 'weirdo' astrologer or pseudo-occultist is, once removed from his narrow band of associates and friends, invariably a figure of hilarity, pity or contempt. It is up to each of us to appraise with honesty just how much of this tendency we have within ourselves.

It might also be worth remembering that genuine character is not created or enhanced by appearance and attitude. If you are an interesting person and have something wonderful like astrology to offer the world, you do not need to cultivate a particularly outstanding or eccentric image. It is usually the transparently fake mystic, whose main intent is merely to provide themselves with an unusual and attractive veneer of occultism and fascination, who is the first to advertise the fact by outward appearance. The real thing has no need of display.

172

You may feel that to bring matters of personal appearance into this is to descend into preaching. But we all have to live in the real world, and the demonstration of a willingness to meet society, with all its faults and imperfections, at least halfway is a sign that others generally respect and, most important of all, trust.

The Invalid's Tale

Yes, astrologers amateur or professional are only human, prone to 'the thousand natural shocks that flesh is heir to.' Inevitably, when your foot is in plaster, or your car in for body repairs, when you lose your job or your house, or all together, some smart aleck is going to ask why you didn't see it coming. The crystal ball will seem to have broken down and, oh dear, how ironic! It becomes a joke as old as the notice outside the fortune-teller's hut on the pier ... 'Sorry. Closed Due to Unforeseen Circumstances'.

Yes, it can be embarrassing but, as most astrologers know from bitter experience, when life's little accidents come along they are rarely totally unexpected. It is often the case that you have located in your chart a particularly unpleasant period ahead but are unable to pinpoint exactly the field of effect. Something nasty is likely to happen, but what exactly is almost impossible to determine. Locking yourself indoors for six weeks or so while the offending planetary configuration passes is hardly a practical solution. Hence it often seems as though you have been taken unawares.

Not to worry. There are plenty of ways around this. Firstly, you can try your best to employ a reputable astrologer in the first place, or if you already are a professional, make sure you forecast your own affairs accurately. Of course, if you have a busy schedule this can be something of a chore, so it might be worth the effort to arrange a reciprocal forecast every once in a while with another astrologer, as it is undoubtedly much easier to forecast for somebody else than for oneself. Such an arrangement would be of value and interest to both parties.

Failing that, the best solution is, again, to practise humility. An astrologer who does not glory in personal powers during the good times is less likely to be the butt of teasing or ridicule when faced with personal problems and misfortunes during the bad. Also, there are one or two good replies that can be directed against anyone who is being especially vindictive. When they ask why it was that you didn't see it coming, simply look them up and down calmly and answer, 'What makes you think I didn't?' A slightly enigmatic attitude here will work wonders. If the adversary is tenacious, however, and insists that, even if you did know, you should have taken steps to prevent it, you will need to explain things a little more fully. Your reply need not be a long soliloquy on the vagaries of fate and free will. Just remind your adversary that to insulate oneself against the bad things in life is also to shut out the good. In other words, the hard times are all part of the package. You believe in meeting life head on with courage. Simple as that.

The Rebel's Tale

A further note of caution has to be sounded in terms of political gullibility and the tendency for astrology to appear 'esoteric' and mildly anti-establishment. Does this ring any bells?

It is perhaps natural to expect an astrologer to be conscious of social issues but someone genuinely open-minded will rarely take such interests to an extreme. The extremist, on the other hand, can be drawn to astrology, particularly to natal and mundane astrology, and those who slip into the habit of using this as a ready-made political platform are perhaps the most obvious offenders. It is here that the golden rule of chart interpretation, that personal preferences and prejudices should never under any circumstances interfere with judgement, is neglected at our peril.

If you are a customer, it is easy to spot this type, since he or she usually makes the worst kind of astrologer. Their interest in you is likely to be more in your degree of social or political awareness rather than any personal matter you may wish to discuss. This attitude filters through into their written work as well: an enduring medium by which the profession will normally be judged. Always you will find the same implicit bias against the evils of capitalism or the dangers of science and technology, always the same smug irony, the same disenchantment with anything remotely connected with law or authority or the mythical bourgeoisie. Astrology really takes second place for these practitioners, and they should be avoided at all costs.

Nor are the rebels among the astrological community going to endear themselves to the vast majority of people by constantly voicing, in their journals and at their conferences, vague cynical opinions pertaining to the so-called 'crises' in science. Science, to the extent that most of us perceive it, is hardly in crisis. The method of reasoning, experimentation and projection of rational scientific values into our daily lives continues to be responsible for an almost unbelievable increase in our well-being and happiness, our health and our liberty.

Slinging mud at science is not going to make astrology shine. And if there are subtle difficulties at the elevated levels of unified field theory or particle physics that challenge traditional materialistic views, it is hardly the place for an astrologer to smugly point them out as if these in some way condone simple irrationality in whatever rough and ready, arbitrary form he or she chooses to present it. The ordinary people in the street know nothing of such subtleties. They are, on the whole, rather happy and pleased with what science has done. And for them such complaints can only be redolent of some medieval inquisition.

It is, again, up to each of us to examine the extent to which we allow internal inadequacies to politically colour our astrology, inadequacies such as frustrated vanity, the desire to be known as vaguely anarchic, or to appear a little bit 'dangerous' and a trifle more exciting and interesting than would otherwise be the case. It really is vitally important for us all to be aware of this danger. For if anything is likely to render astrology laughable and batten it down to the lunacies and irrationalities of the past, it would be an extreme political philosophy which itself may be no more than a grotesque anachronism in the eyes of the vast majority of rational balanced men and women.

The Name-Dropper's Tale

It is often tempting, when arguing for astrology to bring forth the names of distinguished individuals who have supported the subject in the past or actually practised it themselves. The list in Part One (see page 39) provides you with some of these but for reasons of discretion, you will find few contemporary names included. In any case, unless you are absolutely certain that a particular living person, famous or not, explicitly favours astrology, you should not under any circumstances cite his or her name in debate. You may well be correct in saying that such-and-such a person is pro-astrology but you may also be let down later by a denial from that very same individual. This will make you look foolish indeed. Remember, the more prominent a person is the less he or she will wish to have their personal beliefs aired in public, while the professional astrologer should, of course, never disclose the names of his or her clients to anyone, for any purpose. Quoting the names of people who share your views is hardly a satisfactory form of argument in any case, and even if you do stick to historical personages, beware of name-dropping too freely. A clever and erudite opponent may be able to respond with quotations by one or two of the names you have mentioned that seem to doubt or even criticise astrology. This is often as much due to semantics as anything else, confusion arising over precisely what the word 'astrology' or 'astronomy' meant to the writer or speaker in question.

To illustrate this point, we can take two quotations from the

writings of Johannes Kepler (1571–1630). One of the most important figures in the history of astronomy, and indeed of science, Kepler was also an astrologer. His first publication, *De Fundamentis Astrologiae Certioribus*, of 1602, was entirely in support of the astrological hypothesis. In its genuine state, astrology remained a lifelong interest for Kepler, though conventional scholars are rather distressed by this fact, and often quote from Kepler's works and letters in order to unearth a supposedly anti-astrological stance: 'No one should regard it as impossible that, from the follies and blasphemies of astrologers, may emerge a sound and useful body of knowledge.' Or, still more damning, 'Astrology – the foolish daughter, selling herself to maintain the wise mother of astronomy.'[2]

In order to put these two quotations into perspective it is necessary to remember two important things: firstly, that pop astrology and the casting of cheap horoscopes was as prevalent in Kepler's day as it is in our own, and secondly that these quotes, in translation, reflect the attitude of the translator to the way he would like to think of Kepler behaving, as the founder of modern astronomy, rather than a man who busied himself with Pythagoean metaphysics. The original German has the adjective 'buhlerische' to describe the daughter, which does not mean foolish at all, but something closer to 'wanton'. In other words, Kepler may have thought of popular astrology as wasteful but certainly not foolish.

Also, we have to realise that for Kepler astronomy was a science vastly different to the subject that goes by that name today. Astronomy, for this highly original and inventive man, was in fact an elevated and refined form of astrology, a science that could describe the living, mathematical cosmos but which could also reflect the high metaphysical ideals of antiquity and of the European Renaissance. The 'wise mother' in this case was not the astronomy of dry lifeless facts and figures that now confront us in the textbooks of our universities but was in fact astrology with a scientific mathematical content, a perfect synthesis of the physical and metaphysical worlds.

In other cases, quotations may be thrown back at you from venerable historical figures such as Ficino, Augustine or Aquinas. All these men were at times ambivalent to astrology. They were disturbed by the tendency for astrology to seem fatalistic, especially when practised 'wantonly', as Kepler might have put it, without the natural mystical content of Neo-Platonism or early Christianity. Often, they were required to make statements of an anti-astrological nature for purely diplomatic or doctrinal reasons. Often, too, such men would lose their taste for radical ideas in old age when intellectual quietism had set in.

Be prepared for these inconsistencies, and do not be deterred by them. Human beings are complicated things, and opinions and beliefs often change dramatically within the space of one lifetime. Indeed, such change is frequently an indication of an open mind and a developing psyche. Generally it is not advisable, therefore, to stake your case wholly on the sympathetic attitude of any one historical figure. Some of the people in our list will have led foolish and quite appalling lives. In any case, astrology can provide ample protection and evidence in its own right without needing to draw continually on historical precedents. Certainly these can add weight to any defence but do not rely on them for a shield.

Finally, a word about conventional scholars, especially from the earlier part of the twentieth century who have often been bitterly antagonistic towards astrology. An educated opponent may do a little name-dropping of his or her own occasionally; figures such as Neugebauer, Eisler, and so on, may be cited in discussion or correspondence. Unfortunately, some of the best source books on the history of astronomy often contain numerous and heavily laboured comments by these gentlemen against what are seen as the superstitions and follies of the past. Persona is at stake here once again, transparently so, and a kind of nervous, apologetic tone pervades their works whenever astrological references need to be made, the writers having to overstate constantly the fact that they do not give any credence to such tedious details as the zodiac or the mystical origins of astronomy, etc. Often, too, the authors in question have not studied practical astrology sufficiently to be able to pass judgement and their descriptions of the subject often contain inaccuracies and mistakes.

So, while it is wrong, and certainly not wise to denigrate any work of scholarship, do not be impressed if your opponent quotes from such sources as a means towards criticising astrology. If he or she needs to resort to such second-hand tactics, their argument might well be flawed and you should be able to overcome them without too much difficulty.

Happily, today, the situation has improved. Even conventional writers on astronomy manage to treat its great ancestor astrology with some of the respect it deserves, and for every embittered scholar who has railed against the subject in the past, there are now many who approach it with fairness and equanimity.[3]

The Guru's Tale

The would-be astrologer looking for a sensational image is also prey to one other great enemy and opponent that we have not dealt with as yet: the well meaning but rather naïve 'fan' or admirer. Don't be flattered by people who hang on your every word as if it were about to be carved in stone. Being seen to bask in adulation and to feed on the weaknesses of others will not raise your reputation one bit – in fact quite the reverse.

'Just do what needs to be done.
Never take advantage of power.
Achieve results,
But do not glory in them.
Achieve results,
But never boast.'[4]

There is yet a further danger for the guru astrologer: simply frightening people off. Of course you can decide to specialise on the spiritual level, and maybe your clients or friends will respond to that. You can welcome your visitors into a darkened room, light the joss sticks and introduce them immediately to your disembodied guide on the astral plane if you like – but remember, if you are in professional practice, the average man or woman coming to visit you for the first time is likely to be

nervous. They have a right to expect you to behave sensibly and, at least for the time being, reasonably. If you are genuinely psychic, and you cannot resist using your abilities during a sitting, at least explain to your client the various sources of your information or predictions. Tell them that you are using other tools in addition to astrology. Otherwise, if you get it wrong, astrology will take the blame – and this is simply not fair on the profession as a whole.

So instead of ego-tripping, always try to be understanding, firm and honest with your clients and your admirers. Impress on them how astrology has to be approached in a spirit of realism and caution, and remember, too, that you are simply an ordinary representative of the art as it stands today and not some kind of prophet or messianic figure of the Aquarian Age.

The Nerd's Tale

There is a new phenomenon at large in the astrological world today, which would not have been possible before the widespread availability of computers. It's called information overload, and anybody familiar with the vices as well as the virtues of computer technology will be well familiar with the term – and its consequences. Whereas once upon a time the simple astrologer would have happily relied on a basic natal chart which would have been calculated by hand, showing the Sun, Moon and planets, along with a progressed chart or two to furnish themselves and their clients with information and forecasting, they can now step up to the computer and run off literally hundreds of charts in a matter of minutes. Encouraged by the software makers and their bid for ever more elaborate and expensive programs, this, in turn, has led to a proliferation of all manner of quirky astrological tools, making use of mind-bending mathematical contortions that no one would have had time to even contemplate, let alone bother to calculate several years ago.

Now cometh the computer – and wow! We can now do converse tertiary progressions, we can track the movements of every asteroid known to humankind and project them on to the ecliptic; we can examine every fixed star in the firmament for signs of astrological life – and we can even invent totally hypothetical planets, create thousands of hypothetical points if we wish, in order to reveal strange statistical quirks or some remote correlation with events that occur on the world stage. Astrological journals abound with articles speculating on what exactly all of this, or *any of it* could possibly mean – all peppered liberally with wise-after-the-event happenings and accompanied by a bewildering profusion of charts to bedazzle the reader. It seems that we are being urged to believe that even if you cannot find a correlation between astrological doctrine and a certain event, you might well be able to come up with something if you continue producing enough charts!

The 'nerd' is a term given to an archetypal computer buff, and usually summons up visions of adolescents, shut off from the real world for hours on end in front of their computer screens. The entry of the nerd into astrology is a danger – don't go there! Astrology works best when it focuses on the basic bodies of the solar system. If a chart doesn't work with these, it isn't worth asking the computer to solve the problem for you by turning it inside out or by adding any more in number. Computers can be a boon; they can speed up calculations and lighten the load of the working professional immeasurably. But as a means of explaining astrology to the public they can at best be a distraction, at worst a total turn off. (See the next chapter for a look at the significantly unspectacular effects that computers and statistical research have had on the public imagination in recent times.)

Are there any more cautionary tales? Probably as many as there are astrologers to tell them. By the nature of the subject you will be functioning in pretty rarefied air, up high, where there is always the possibility of a fall. Do not worry. Go ahead and be what you are, and remember that fortune favours the brave.

CHAPTER 11

Lies, Damned Lies and Statistics

In recent years there has been a good deal of activity in the area of astrological research, which, inevitably, makes liberal use of statistics. This is something which, for good or bad, seems likely to continue – especially with the ready availability of powerful computers. The statistician, too, is undoubtedly here to stay, and so everyone interested in astrology should perhaps be familiar with at least a smattering of these topics in order to become a true all-round competitor in the art of self-defence.

The statement, often made, that you can prove anything with statistics is perhaps a rather smug and cynical one. Such technical understanding is a great aid and support in our search for knowledge and awareness of the world in which we live, and there is no reason why astrologers, too, should not employ statistics occasionally to demonstrate their claims or to defend themselves when challenged at that level. However, remember that a good astrologer has no more need of statistics to justify his or her position than has, say, an accomplished artist, a political leader or a good friend. The deeds, the thoughts and the simple integrity of such people are sufficient. Nor do all astrologers necessarily believe statistical research to be useful or even desirable. Opinions differ widely.

In addition to this, a state of warfare now seems to exist between astrologers and certain sections of the scientific community – and this, too, shows no signs of abating any time soon. It is difficult to know who actually first commenced hostilities but some scientists, in the face of astrology's increasing popularity, have felt the need to hit back with one or two emotional outbursts of quite amazing intemperance and irrationality.

For example, as far back as 1975 it was thought prudent for a group of scientists to publish a kind of public rebuttal of the subject. This took the form of a statement, drafted by astronomer Bart Bok and signed by 186 'leading' scientists that appeared in the American magazine *Humanist*. The statement, which was also circulated to many newspapers and periodicals, urged its readers to consider the evils and perils of astrology and the impossibility of it possessing any rational scientific foundation.[1] The response of astrologers was to publish their own counter-declaration, signed not by 186 but by 187 academically distinguished people who were either astrologers themselves or else believed the subject to present a valid area for investigation and research.[2]

So, a kind of childish tit-for-tat exchange had already emerged, the first statement based, as many people felt, on hysteria and a total lack of empirical evidence or understanding, and the second, although far more reasonable in tone, being almost equally as paranoid. The battle had begun. Astrology had entered the world of modern warfare. The fact that it all seemed so much bluster, rather like the small boys in the playground not being allowed to play with the big boys, was beside the point. Egos were at stake, the persona of the professional was threatened. Astrologers and scientists alike began to squirm and squabble as though their very existence depended on sustaining their own particular claims and prejudices. Partly in response to this, there is now an organisation in the States, with branches world-wide, that goes by the name of the Committee for the Scientific Investigation into Claims of the Paranormal (CSICOP), and which regularly takes a swipe at all things metaphysical through its journals and websites. As the acronym suggests, CSICOP is perceived by many as a kind of self-styled 'thought police', shielding the citizens of our modern society from the perils of darkness and superstition. Astrologers are fair game, of course, and are even made fun of. The very idea! Some astrologers find this sort of thing infuriating, especially at those times when they believe they have some kind of proof to announce to the world. To date, the squabbles continue unabated.

A major hang-up suffered by certain sections of the astrological community and highlighted with ruthless regularity by CSICOP is the existence of an embarrassing credibility gap. The proof just isn't there in a scientific sense. Yet still the astrologers in question cannot quite bring themselves to give up on the idea that it ought to be, or could be one day if only those stubborn scientists would change their ways and be a little more accommodating. It's a tough call, though – because science remains a distinctly dominant animal. It thrives on two major sources of sustenance: experimentation and verification. In science, proof is everything – a principle that is sacrosanct. A scientific hypothesis, demonstrated successfully a hundred times can be destroyed by a single failure, whereas astrology is often seen by its critics to flourish in a climate where a single successful prediction can cancel out a hundred failures. Quite a difference. In fact, the art of astrology does not compare at all well with science for one very good reason: the paramount importance of interpretation and human judgement – qualities central to the working core of astrology and which cannot be quantified in a scientific sense at all. The notion, therefore, that astrology is a budding science, a poor relative of physics, engineering or biology, just waiting in the wings ready to be transformed into a formal white-coated technology is rightly seen as absurd.

Where, then, does all this leave astrology now during the opening years of the twenty-first century? Still undaunted and doggedly determined is the answer. We continue to see numerous experiments, ingenious attempts at statistical analysis of astrology, both for and against the subject. With few exceptions, however, these have proved hopelessly inadequate. Meanwhile, there are more and more dedicated journals, prestigious conferences, lengthy correspondences that go on for years, all to no avail. No sooner does some brave astrologer come up with proof that astrology actually works, than somebody else – often another astrologer – brings out a paper demonstrating that he, or she, is, in fact, wrong and that the work is flawed in some sense. An argument ensues, lots of conflicting interpretations of the results are bandied about and everyone gets very upset with everyone else; astrology is not improved much as a consequence, and the whole thing dies a natural death – until the next time.

The basic problem until recently was that astrologers were poor statisticians, while statisticians themselves were weak in their understanding of the subtle mechanisms of astrology – sometimes purposely so. To illustrate some of these difficulties in real terms, we will look firstly at two experiments from the heyday of astrological debate, one in favour of astrology, and the other against. And although there have been plenty of attempts to square the circle since then, these two very different pieces of work from the closing decades of the last century encapsulate the errors and the prejudices ranged on both sides of the debate which, sadly, have not really changed much since they first saw light.

In the late 1960s the distinguished British astrologer Jeff Mayo, founder of one of the foremost colleges for training astrologers and a noted writer on the subject, initiated an experiment on zodiac signs and the way in which each sign's polarity, positive or negative, might relate to individual character. To this end, a number of people were asked to assess their own personality through a questionnaire that was, in turn, compared with the volunteers' Sun signs.[3]

The degrees of extraversion or introversion indicated by these questionnaires were then projected on to the six positive and six negative Sun signs of the zodiac, traditionally associated with extraversion and introversion respectively. This subsequently revealed an amazing correlation between the personalities and the signs. Those born under the positive signs of Aries, Gemini, Leo, and so on, returned questionnaires which were on balance plainly extraverted, while the subjects born under the negative signs of Taurus, Cancer, Virgo, and so on, really did come across as the deep, introverted types. The problem with this experiment, as it later transpired, was that many of the subjects participating in the research were taken from among Jeff Mayo's own students, who were already familiar with Sun-sign doctrine and hence the exact level of introversion/extraversion that might be expected of them when filling out the questionnaires. And although Jeff Mayo's colleagues and others have since undertaken far more sophisticated and encouraging work in this field, his oversight in this case was typical of those committed by researchers early on, when they were not yet familiar with the rigours of statistical analysis. Experiment invalid.

On the other side of the fence, in 1985 an experiment, conducted at the Department of Physics, Berkeley, was published in the scientific journal Nature. The experiment, it was claimed, disproved astrology.[4] Indeed, reading the introduction and the concluding remarks of the paper, one would have to admit the author had succeeded admirably in doing just that. Studying the experiment itself, however, left the impartial observer in some doubt. Apparently, even a member of the original research team felt they had to resign early owing to an inherent bias in the experiment itself that was almost guaranteed to produce negative results.[5]

A complex experiment, featuring a double-blind test, it began with a group of volunteers who were each asked to complete a questionnaire called a CPI, which is short for California Personality Inventory. The CPI produces a character profile of a highly specialised kind, intelligible only to trained psychologists. The CPIs, plus two other 'fake' control ones for each volunteer, were then sent with the necessary birth data to a number of participating astrologers (who really should have known better) with the requirement that without any personal contact with the volunteers themselves they cast a birth chart for each one and then try to pick out the correct CPIs. In other words, could the astrologer match the correct character profile to its owner's horoscope?

At the same time the astrologers were obliged to write character analyses for these charts, based on their own interpretations, and return these to the examiners. These were in turn presented for each volunteer's appraisal, along with two other 'fake' control interpretations. Each volunteer was then required to pick out the one most closely resembling his or her own personality.

Unfortunately, a little earlier, when asked to pick out their own CPIs based on the original personality test, the subjects had great difficulty in doing so – such was the accuracy and relevance of the CPIs themselves without the necessary expert analysis for which they were designed. Because of this difficulty, the second half of the experiment was scrapped. The earlier part, however, the astrologers' contribution, was retained, and results were produced showing that they were, statistically, unable to use their astrological skills to pick out the correct CPIs from the controls any more than chance would normally allow.

How the poor astrologers were supposed to select the correct CPIs when even the people to whom they belonged were unable to do so is puzzling. Nevertheless, this was cited as conclusive proof that the astrological hypothesis had been refuted. A further slant to the experiment was that the sex of each volunteer was not included in the data presented to the astrologers – this being one of the most vital pieces of information needed, not only for any worthwhile astrological analysis, but also for the correct interpretation of the CPI! This is certainly 'science' at its least persuasive.

Fortunately, human character is rather more complex than the mere delineation and outcome of personality tests which – even when designed to be more 'user-friendly' than the CPI – are still normally filled out by the volunteers in person who tend, therefore, to gloss over any character faults in favour of a glowing description of themselves. The astrologer is then supposed to match these to a chart that will, of course, generally show the whole truth. Thus the discrepancy inevitably arises and pronouncements are made that 'astrology doesn't work'. None of this should be at all surprising to anyone who has studied human nature but it might come as a shock to others engaged in more specialised fields. Experiment invalid.

Michel Gauquelin

Statistics can be used creatively and intelligently however, and when they are they constitute a useful part of the modern armament, for both astrologer and – sadly – cynics alike. It is necessary therefore to be aware of the successes in this field, particularly the work of the French statistician and psychologist Michel Gauquelin (pronounced rather like Cork-a-lan, by the way). A small book of this nature can hardly do justice to the work of this dedicated and tenacious man, but we should at least be able to draw our opponents' attention to the basic results of his work if we are ever challenged from a purely technical or scientific standpoint. As you might already have noticed, I have cited Gauquelin's research frequently in Part Two. It deserves to be mentioned here as well, however, and needs to be looked at in more detail. It is a remarkable body of work, and many people believe that even now it has not been surpassed.

Over the years, Gauquelin studied many thousands of charts, and submitted them to rigorous and exhaustive statistical analysis. In this he was particularly successful in isolating a high frequency of strong planetary placements in the charts of eminent professionals such as athletes, doctors, actors, and so on. In this context, a planet is considered strong when it is rising, setting or crossing the upper or lower meridian of the birth

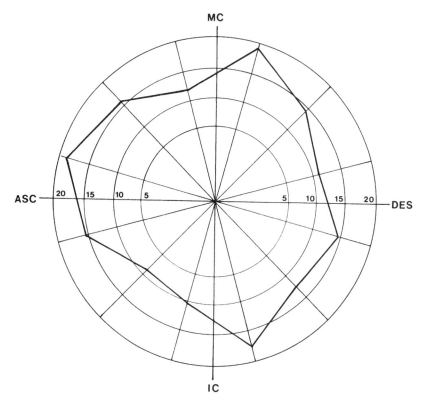

Figure 7. An example of the way that astrological statistics may be presented

chart. Gauquelin's results were remarkable. For instance, the traditionally energetic and aggressive planet Mars was shown to be more frequently strong in the charts of eminent sportsmen than chance would normally allow. The same was true of other planets and other professions: Jupiter for politicians, Saturn for scientists, and the Moon for writers. These professional attributes tended, moreover, to be in line with traditional astrological lore which had always associated Mars with competitive spirit, Jupiter with politics, Saturn with concentration, the Moon with imagination, and so on.[6]

Refer to Figure 7 (see above) for an example of the way this kind of data is presented. The chart shown is basically a graph turned into a circle – sometimes called a radar or a spiderweb chart – so that the larger and larger circles emanating from the

189

centre like ripples on a pool indicate frequency, or number, while the circumference of the circle itself represents the 360 degrees of the sky. The 'chart' here is therefore a composite of all the birth charts examined in one particular test, superimposed, one over the other on to one 'mean' chart. There are twelve different sectors marked out for examination here, rather like the houses in a normal astrological chart. A solid line is then plotted between each sector showing the number of 'hits' for the particular planet under consideration. Clearly there is a peak around the Ascendant and the MC of the charts examined. The planet in question appears in these sectors far more often, when examining a group of charts, than in the other sectors, and the chances against this are extremely remote unless astrology is, indeed, a reality.

Although, sadly, some of Gauquelin's other studies failed to confirm any additional features of traditional astrological lore, his work did reveal one other startling fact – a special relationship between the birth charts of parents and children. If a certain planet, say Jupiter, was strong in the chart of any one or both of the parents, then there was, he found, an above average chance of it being so in the chart of the child. But, as we have already seen, this applies to natural births only. When births are forced or manipulated the effect disappears.[7] This discovery of a natural hereditary/planetary link is perhaps one of the most startling and relevant findings of all. The social significance is quite staggering.

Over the years these experiments have been expanded and replicated, and the work continues. However, do note that occasionally those hostile to Gauquelin and astrology have replicated the experiments in an incomplete or, some say, biased fashion and produced inconclusive findings. These have usually outraged impartial observers and have been the subject of much scandal and bickering.[8] The most common ploy in these replication experiments is to choose birth data of those not especially eminent in their respective professions: the also-rans of sport, for example. Naturally the astrological correlations of the original research disappear in these cases. The 'eminence effect', as it has been termed, is essential to this kind of research and the conclusions of Gauquelin have been reinforced more often than they have been unjustly refuted.[9]

It must be pointed out, moreover, that Gauquelin's discovery, or rather confirmation of particularly planetary features, is but a minute part of the overall system of astrological usage, most of which still remains unproven – which is perhaps why even he remained uncommitted to the usefulness of his own findings. Obviously he did accept certain factors – his 'Mars effect' for example – but until a more comprehensive body of proof was on hand for the other tenets of astrology (and there are many yet to be examined) he cautiously reserved judgement, exemplifying the true spirit of scientific and empirical research, something which many of his critics would have done well to emulate. Sadly he died in 1991.

Enter the Neofatalists

Encouraged by the results obtained by Gauquelin and others, statistical research remains a fashionable subject within the serious astrological community, promising rewards of approval and acceptance undreamed of since the Enlightenment. And despite warnings from other, perhaps less divinely discontented astrologers, that the subject does not lend itself to reductionist study, experiments abound. The warnings emphasise that the business of astrology is only intelligible when each of the many separate factors is blended and synthesised into a meaningful whole, usually involving the intelligence of a human being. However, astrology's champions of research still persist in isolating single discrete factors such as sun signs, or single aspects, or positive/negative polarity, and then setting up statistical programs to relate these to traits such as physical dexterity, genius, propensity to crime, suicide, and so on.

Enthusiasm for such work is fuelled by the statistical axiom that providing you take a large enough sample of subjects, then even a weak, isolated factor should eventually show up in the figures – like a tendency for more soldiers to be born when the Sun is in the martial sign of Aries, or other simplistic arguments of that nature. Those astrologers who are aware of the reductionist dilemma tend to view this as rather an odd notion however, one which seems to infer that, although two wrongs do not necessarily make a right, several thousand might – if you stick at it long enough. Sadly, results when they have occurred have invariably failed to stand up to the most important aspect of statistical doctrine, that of replication. Many of the arguments on which experimentation is based turn out to be both naïve and prejudiced, so that seemingly trivial technical points often destroy the basis of the project itself.

This is also the case when attempts are valiantly made to do what are termed whole-chart or global studies, which, for example, may feature the examination of anonymous charts, which are then related back to their owners through normal procedures of interpretation and synthesis. In other words, can the astrologers match the birth charts to the personalities of their owners without knowing who they are? The Berkeley experiment mentioned earlier was a rather sophisticated example of this kind.

Here, as we have seen, difficulty inevitably arises in establishing an independent measure of the personalities of the volunteers. In addition to the CPI there are other personality tests such as the EPQ (Eysenck Personality Questionnaire) and others that are used in such experiments, but – as astrologer's themselves have pointed out – these have the major flaw of being open not necessarily to fraud but to self-delusion on the part of those volunteers who fill them out. As we have already seen, many of the so-called failures of statistical research can be traced to the impracticality of asking people to judge and then to fill out their own personality profile or – perhaps even worse – asking their friends or relatives to do so.

Die hard enthusiasts of statistical research are resourceful beasts, however, and experiments have been designed to get around this to a certain extent – so, for example, the astrologer is asked to relate the charts to other more concrete features such as profession. Is it possible to locate the chart for the librarian, or the one for the musician? The answer is sometimes yes, to a degree at least, with results better than chance would normally allow. There were quite a number of such exercises during the latter half of the last century – the experiments of Vernon Clark (1961 and 1970), Dobyns (1975 and 1976) and Vidmar (1979)[10] and more recently work by the distinguished German statistician Suitbert Ertel 1998.[11] Often, though, the data and method of these experiments have been criticised or, in the case of Ertel the study failed to show up any statistical significance. In this last instance, birth data for twenty politicians and twenty painters

were given to astrologers to distinguish one from the other.
Perhaps not surprising in a world where human beings are
inevitably more complex than the mere delineation of their
profession, the results were inconclusive. One must assume that
Winston Churchill was not among those chosen for consideration
(having been both painter and politician – and a whole lot more,
of course.)

Undeterred by these rather disappointing results, however,
researchers still continue to design and run experiments of the
same sort. Often, too, the experiments are conducted by those
seeking to disprove astrology (see pages 166–67), and the
negative results are gleefully displayed for public consumption.
Whether pro or anti astrology, studies of this kind remain
inevitably flawed because they do not reflect the way astrology
functions in the real world. In practice, astrologers and clients
ͬ ᴜally work together, sharing information. There is normally
some form of personal contact, too, either through an interview,
a phone conversation or an e-mail. Clients are expected to share
information concerning their background and family, their
profession, their wishes and aspirations with the astrologer so
that he or she can tailor the work accordingly. An ongoing
relationship is often built up over time. And no one, but *no one* is
ever in the business of guessing things.

Not all statistical work falls flat, however. And in addition to
the work of Gauquelin, there have in recent times appeared one
or two relatively encouraging pieces of research that have
produced results. Although not earth-shattering in their
findings, these studies do demonstrate that there is something
unusual going on that cannot be simply brushed aside. For
example, in the year 2000, where sociability was measured from
among a group of as many as 524 students and related back to
the solar position within the positive and negative signs of the
zodiac at birth. This – a more sophisticated version of the Mayo
experiment described earlier – really did seem to validate the
polarity effect of the zodiac signs.[12] In another recent experiment
from Kollerstrom and Steffert in 2003, four years' worth of
telephone call frequency data was obtained from a crises call
centre and then correlated to the lunar cycle. Here, it was found
that there was a statistically significant increase in calls recorded
from females during the New Moon period. This is particularly

interesting, since in astrology the Moon is typically related to the female sex and to emotions generally. Without dividing the data by sex in this way, the effect would have been more or less invisible. But once the sex of the callers was clarified it appeared that, indeed, distress calls by women were more strongly linked to the monthly lunar cycle than were those by men.[13]

On a more popular level, there has always been the kind of experiment in which a panel of astrologers is asked to guess, and often succeeds in guessing the Sun signs of various individuals after a brief interview. This might, for example, be a televised experiment. And – again – results are often better than chance would allow. However, all these experiments have been criticised owing to their basic lack of practical value. An element of clever guesswork or even ESP could have been operative at the time, or any other number of non-astrological clues – 'artefacts' as they are called in statistical jargon. And, as one commentator has already remarked, these experiments do not necessarily demonstrate that astrology works but only that *astrologers* do.

It is also possible that the rather unsavoury nature of such 'party tricks' could ultimately damage astrology itself, because the natural extension of such an attitude would be experiments in which, say, the astrologers are given a dozen charts of murderers and a dozen of law-abiding citizens with instructions to distinguish which charts belong to which. Fortunately, no one has yet been able to make this kind of distinction from the examination of birth data alone. Moreover, the idea that this could in some way be possible is an appalling one that utterly negates the fundamental principle of free will and moral integrity. Does a person have no choice as to whether he or she becomes a murderer or a librarian? And if a person does have a choice, why bother to submit the birth chart to statistical analysis in the first place?

Surely any man or woman is much more than a passive projection of their horoscope at birth or – mercifully – of their profession! This should be obvious to all, and yet for many the paradox of statistical astrology remains invisible. On the one hand they assert, as do all respectable astrologers, that free will is paramount to the interpretation and workings of any individual chart. Yet on the other they maintain that certain horoscopic factors exert influence detectable by statistics and which experts can spot instantly, as though picking out rotten apples from a barrel. If this is so, then astrologers can safely kiss goodbye to any pretence at being free of fatalistic dogma. Instead, the destinies of whole groups of people become subordinate to the trivial factors that statisticians have supposedly isolated in their charts.

As an enthusiast of astrology, you will need to be aware of this paradox, and of the mistakes still being made today by those who try to turn astrology into a quantifiable science, for by so doing they will also have to turn human nature into one. This is not only an appalling proposition, but also an impossible one. It is debatable, therefore, whether we can ever further astrology through reductionism and statistical research of this kind. We cannot have free will as well as cut-and-dried astrological correlations. We can't have it both ways – and perhaps it is time we woke up to this fact and returned to interpreting charts for whole people and not just bits of them.

For the moment, however, this is unlikely to happen. Statistical research continues to attract some of the best minds in the profession. A leading commentator on all things statistical in the astrological world estimated recently that from a mere handful of studies in astrological and psychological journals in the middle of the last century, the number of empirical studies had, by 2003, reached in excess of five hundred! Evidence is passionately sought after, a burning thirst for scientific respectability, gaining more and more momentum with every new flick of the computer on-switch. The idea seems to be that now statistical proof of a few basic fragments of astrological lore has been demonstrated, it is surely only a matter of time before the scientific establishment sees the potential of the subject, takes it into the hallowed halls of its universities and research labs and begins throwing inordinate sums of money at it. So far, however, things have not quite worked out that way.

These neofatalists of the astrological community, who forget that scientists are people too, with pride, fears and anxieties just like anyone else are not going to do themselves much good by waving statistics in their faces just in order to prove a handful of astrological commonplaces, which are, ultimately, of little practical use. Scientists are not overly pleased when someone borrows the tools of their trade in order, as they see it, to discredit the foundations of their belief and purpose – because that is precisely what astrology, if proven, would do. Moreover, trying to muscle in on the periphery of the big boy's game may actually have been instrumental in whipping up the hostility of the scientific establishment in the first place. It also has to be seriously open to question whether astrology needs to join the science game at all. Astrology is already so rich and comprehensive a subject – embracing, as it does, the whole spectrum of mankind's creative, religious, artistic and psychological aspirations – that to waste time and energy paying homage to the scientific establishment seems decidedly superfluous.

Conclusion

To conclude this chapter, which admittedly has been largely concerned with sounding a note of caution regarding statistical research in astrology, I think we can relent just a little – because, oddly enough, and for all the hundreds of studies that have taken place, most of them providing inconclusive evidence for some kind of 'proof' of astrology, the most interesting statistic of all can perhaps be gleaned from a simple look at the *Sunday Times* Rich List, which is published annually and which also includes a Sun-sign breakdown of Britain's 1000 wealthiest individuals or families.

The list for 2004 actually contained 1,100 individuals in all and, of these, 1,067 had their Sun-signs recorded – so nearly all of them. Bearing in mind that there are just the twelve signs, a sceptic of astrology would expect there to be a more-or-less equal distribution of 1,067 divided by 12 people for each one – that is, around 89 (give or take just a little due to the different lengths of time the Sun actually stays in each sign). In fact, it was revealed that as many as 110 were born under 'clever' Gemini but only 73 under 'dreamy' Pisces. A huge disparity, but entirely what astrologers and most astrologically informed members of the public would have expected. Critics will, of course, say that much of this is inherited wealth and so the figures mean nothing. In fact, only a small percentage was listed as being inherited. Furthermore, I would draw the attention of any would-be doubters to the universally acknowledged fact that one of the most difficult things about having money, inherited or otherwise, is actually keeping it.

Perhaps astrology's detractors will be able to shoot this one down in flames. I can almost hear the pencils being sharpened already. But I like this piece of information. Best of all I like its simplicity – something that everyone can relate to and understand. This might, indeed, be 'proof' of a kind – and from the most unlikely of sources. (It will do for me.)

So there you have it. Ultimately, statistics can be impressive, admirable: they really do prove things. But rarely is anyone impressed unless the statistics already back up existing opinions or prejudices. This is as true for the academic specialist as it is for the layperson. Interesting astrological statistics mean little to a scientist who has spent a lifetime using them as a tool of atheism or warfare, nor do they mean much to the person who has spent a whole evening winning, inexplicably, at the roulette wheel, who has just won the lottery or been struck by lightning. So astrologers beware! Ultimately, rather than establish security and acceptance, this continuously unrequited love affair with science could in the future only serve to alienate astrology still further from the vast bulk of the general public who, mistakenly it would seem, once regarded it as a study pertaining to human feelings and aspirations, rather than to vast bundles of graphs and equations.

Like astrology itself, statistics enable us to impose order on to the vast and magnificent complexity of nature, to try to unravel the fascinating puzzles that surround us and to help answer some of the unfathomable and often terrible questions about being alive. Unlike astrology, however, which enriches our lives and rejoices in the mystery and infinite subtlety of our world, statistics place a cold, limiting straitjacket upon our imaginations, our independent volition and our dignity. In the way of all temporal laws and systems of measurement and analysis, it suffers from the limitations of reductionism: the whole becomes lost in the search for detail. In the years ahead, it would be a shame if, in order to buy a little transient prestige and rank, astrology needed to descend permanently to that level.

CHAPTER 12

Final Pep Talk

Y
ou have by now at least dipped into this book, hopefully with a view to studying it and learning how to defend yourself in practice. Confidence in the twelve-part form will help with the essential business of improvisation so vital to successful self-defence. Added to this, perhaps the most important ingredient of all, courage or sheer 'bottle', has to be cultivated. For instance, distinguished masters of the martial arts have been known to 'freeze' in moments of real attack, on the street and away from the familiar routine of the gymnasium or club. Knowing the moves is not enough, you have to have the fluency and the strength of your own convictions to be effective.

The sage tells us that 'for the Believer, no proof is necessary; while for the Disbeliever, no proof is possible.' This is a reasonable statement, but there are various shades of grey between these two extremes, and at the back of many an astrologer's mind, particularly the less professionally successful or amateur astrologer, may often lay a nagging insecurity or doubt. 'Is it really right? Does it really work? Am I really on the right track or simply deluding myself?' Every astrologer at some stage in his or her career – or even the dedicated enthusiast of the subject – will have suffered from such doubts. It can happen to the most experienced as well as to the beginner. Often you will compare your aspirations with a distinct lack of practical or tangible results and wonder if there is any authenticity in astrology at all.

This is not only a sad state but also a rather arrogant one, since it supposes that just because you yourself cannot secure tangible or conclusive results, that the entire body of learning and thought that has constituted astrology over the centuries is somehow worthless. This may be understandable at times of personal crises when self-confidence and self-esteem may diminish for a while, but it is just a little conceited. It is also wrong.

If this sounds like you, please don't worry! You are certainly not alone. Apart from your own moments of doubt, you will soon discover, from a simple glance through the various journals, books and papers that proliferate among the astrological community, that nowhere is the validity of modern astrology questioned as frequently and exhaustively as among modern astrologers themselves. Current research and experimentation sets an extremely rigorous standard of verification, while traditional tenets are questioned continuously with a critical attitude verging on mistrust and, sometimes, even contempt. Honesty and integrity as well as those occasional bursts of cynicism and self-doubt abound to such a degree that indeed astrology often seems to be its own worst enemy. Nothing is taken on face value; nothing is sacred.

Well, who can blame us! For the paradox facing the enthusiast of astrology in modern times is as painful as that facing any other thinking, sensitive individual, be they artist, philosopher or theologian: anyone who instinctively adheres to a belief-system based on intangibles, on the feelings, the emotions and the mind. It is the paradox of spirit contending with matter and the cogent world of the senses. In a society where so many values are measured in terms of material evidence and financial reward, it is really only to be expected that this 'inner' experience will be viewed with less importance or even less credibility than the amazing physical presence of, say, your average suspension bridge or microprocessor.

This physical world of machinist miracles has now become the sole testing ground for truth. Can we see it, touch it, feel it? If the answer is no, then it is not real; it is irrelevant. Simple as that. People want and expect results, the surety of the sense-experience before they will listen to your strange ideas. Where is astrology's microchip or satellite receiver to set the senses tingling? We do not have it. And although astrology is a truly Uranian subject, capable of bridging the rifts between the mental, spiritual and physical worlds, it is not likely ever to deal directly in that particular brand of miracles: the 'hard' miracles of the senses.

Do not be intimidated, however. Do not be put off. For the great objective mechanical view of life contains one encouraging paradox once you start to think and question. Matter itself, the logical catalyst around which all our ideas of modern reality have hitherto evolved, has long been shown, through relativity theory and quantum mechanics, to be virtually empty space anyway, merely populated by a number of subtle electrical and magnetic forces. Mass, gravitation, reality itself, it's all just energy – and what energy is no one quite knows. Energy? It's a word, a name, but what's in a name?

Never must you view science as an enemy, therefore. Unlike many of astrology's detractors, those at the apex of the scientific pyramid are often sympathetic to the spirit of life and its creative subtlety. They are people who have been able to lighten up and open their minds to the infinite possibilities of existence, and they are people, too, whose research has often led them to touch upon that very essence of the mystical and the spiritual. Meanwhile, the things that really make the world go around: feelings, ideas, loves and passions, will always be comprehensible only through the great philosophical and theological systems of humanity, within which astrology has always been celebrated and high esteemed.

The secret is not to fall into the trap of doubt, of envy for the machinists and their toy miracles. Admittedly, it might not only be your friends, colleagues or family but also much of the social establishment and economic world view that will seem to be against you at times. Possibly these will be lifelong adversaries, the hard work and dreams of our statisticians notwithstanding. You will simply have to get used to this – for even in the light of recent experiments, such as the work of Gauquelin or Piccardi, and the obvious 'perks' these bring to astrology, the scientific world remains unimpressed, the layperson oblivious. Conventional scholarship has a remarkable talent for absorbing exciting developments such as these, of taking them under its wing and simply flying away. Work of this kind, as with the pioneering discoveries begun by Nelson in the last century, may well be destined to form yet another thread in astronomy's vast network of force fields, electromagnetic, atomic or otherwise, that generally succeeds in explaining away the miraculous.

The soldier's maxim is 'Divide and conquer': the technologist's is 'Name it and conquer'. For how often does the naming of a thing rob it of its magic, its potency as a moving force within the psyche! The self-styled 'sidereal scientists' have already taken the bait. It is sad. Perhaps they should just bear in mind that our cynical godless era is, so far, brief in comparison to the history of humanity. It is likely that a balance of spirit will return in time. Of course, whether this is to be sooner or later depends a lot on us, on people just like you and me.

Now there's an interesting thought!

If you want it to happen, if you believe in progress, then you will already realise just how important the return of equilibrium between spirit and matter is going to be. When it comes, this new balance will have to treat all of life, all ideas and occupations with equal respect, awarding merely varying degrees of cogency to all the wide and varied affairs of humankind – a Spectrum of Certainty, if you like, with the solid manifest wonders of engineering and technology, bridges and skyscrapers, microprocessors and DVDs at one end of the scale and the less tangible elements of life: the arts, love, ecstasy and the metaphysical world of religion and philosophy, towards the other.

This Spectrum of Certainty must admit all aspects of humanity, all facets of being alive, none being superior to the other but each having its place on the scale of physical certainty and regularity. You can predict the results of engineering with almost complete confidence; they are at one end. But the effects of music on the heart come out with far less certainty. Likewise astrology will fit in somewhere on the spectrum; where exactly must depend on the astrologer himself – but it will be, wherever it falls, valid. All things are. Just like the real rainbow spectrum – which is, the physicists tell us, part of a much wider electromagnetic scale which our eyes limit to certain wavelengths only – just like that real rainbow of light, the Spectrum of Certainty will always be limited by our own personal breadth of vision, or that of our race and culture.

Yet it can grow; it can evolve. And that must be where astrology is heading right now: expanding from within. It really is so vast a subject, capable of such breadth and exclusiveness that it extends perhaps further off the scale than most of us can imagine, taking in cultures, religions and the dreams and aspirations of men and women from every walk of life, every corner of the world. Like helpless beasts of burden, we labour under such a yoke of materialism, selfishness and greed in our present age that the very ecology and life-stuff of the world itself is threatened. Astrology provides us all with a common symbolic language which is both stimulating and entertaining, and if we can encourage those around us to use their imaginations occasionally, to lift their noses from the trough and look up at the stars, the outcome can only be positive for all concerned. For this reason alone, your dreams are worth pursuing.

So go ahead – go get it! Don't be discouraged. There is no need to fear anyone, no need to scrape to anybody else. Astrology is worthy enough in its own right. You can best serve astrology by fighting under your own true colours, and, if a professional in the field, you can best demonstrate its validity by simply getting to work ... by being of use to the community and, above all, by becoming continually more and more accurate: by simply being right, and in serving those who come to listen.

Astrology is an idea, perhaps the patriarch in the family of great and magnificent ideas that have continually nourished and shaped humanity. If, indeed, we are all of us astrologers, then we should no more seek to address ourselves to the dull technocrat than to any other specialised representative of society, no more than to the politician or the theologian, the financier or the guru, the industrialist or the child.

Astrology is greater than any one discipline or lifestyle. It is of importance because it touches upon the raw emotive level of life to which everyone, but everyone, ultimately relates, no matter who or what he or she is, no matter what position he or she holds in society. Astrology is totally relevant, therefore, and you must never doubt its worth. It is a direct link to the divine source of all knowledge and experience that progresses and unfolds continually into the future. As it moves, and as you move with it, you will find that it echoes the very metabolism and life stuff of the human body, and therefore the body of humanity also, mind and soul.

I believe it is the North American Indians who have a saying, 'Walk in pride'. Do so, and you will never need to look back.

Notes and References

Chapter 5
1. Lao Tzu, *Tao Te Ching*, trans. Ch'u Ta-Kao, George Allen & Unwin, 1959.

Chapter 7
1. Pagan, I., *Signs of the Zodiac Analysed*, original title of *From Pioneer to Poet*, Theosophical Publishing House, 1911.
2. Gauquelin, M., *The Truth About Astrology*, Basil Blackwell, 1983.

Chapter 8
1. West, J. & Toonder, J., *The Case for Astrology*, Arkana, 1992. Contains some interesting photographs of time twins, though some details in the stories have been discredited by later research.
2. Eysenck, H.J. & Nias, D.K.B., *Astrology, Science or Superstition?* Maurice Temple Smith, 1982.
3. West. J. & Toonder, J., *The Case for Astrology*, Arkana, 1992.
4. ibid.
5. Dean, G. & Mather, A., *Recent Advances in Natal Astrology*, Analogic, Perth, 1977.
6. Roberts, P. & Greengrass, H., *The Astrology of Time Twins*, Bishop Auckland: Pentland Press, 1994.
7. Dean, G. & Mather, A., *Recent Advances in Natal Astrology*, Analogic, Perth 1977.
8. Dean, G. & Kelly, I., *Journal of Consciousness Studies*, 10 no. 6, 2003. See also www.astrologicalassociation.com
9. Gorman, P., *Pythagoras, A Life*, Routledge & Kegan Paul, 1979.
10. Lerner, M., *The Astrological Journal*, XXVIII no. 4. This contains an article describing Lerner's nuclear trigger or axis, and his subsequent predictions of important events related to the atomic industry. In his own periodical, *Welcome to Planet Earth*, Lerner successfully predicted, as early as mid-1983, a major disaster in the nuclear field between late January and mid-May 1986. Regarding the capsizing of the ship *The Herald of Free Enterprise*, in 1987, see *The Astrological Journal*, XXIX no. 3; apparently Dennis Elwell sent a registered letter to the owners of the ship warning of potential danger just days before the tragedy.
11. Crawford Perspectives, the monthly newsletter by Wall Street financial technician Arch Crawford. See June 1990, May 2000 and September 2001.
12. Nostradamus, *The Prophecies of Nostradamus*, Neville Spearman, 1973.
13. Crawford Perspectives, June 1990.
14. Crawford Perspectives, August 1987.
15. *The Astrological Journal*, XXIV no. 4. Swiss Journal, *Cosmotrend*, for Angermeyer.
16. Crawford Perspectives, May 2000 and September 2001.
17. Gleadow, R., *The Origins of the Zodiac*, Jonathan Cape, 1968. And Walters, D., *Chinese Astrology*, Aquarian Press, 1987.

18. Lindsay, J., *Origins of Astrology*, Frederick Muller, 1971.

19. Neugebauer, O., *The Exact Sciences in Antiquity*, Brown University Press, 1957. Contains many interesting illustrations, monuments, tombs, etc. from ancient times.

20. Yates, F., *The Art of Memory*, Routledge & Kegan Paul, 1966.

21. Webb, E., *The Names of the Stars*, Nisbet & Co., London, 1952.

22. Manilius, *Astronomica*, Loeb Edition, Heinemann, London, 1977.

23. Gauquelin, M., *How Cosmic and Atmospheric Energies Influence Your Health*, Aurora Press, New York, 1981.

24. Jung, C., commentary included in *The Secret of the Golden Flower*, the Chinese classic translated by Richard Wilhelm, Routledge & Kegan Paul, 1962.

25. Gauquelin, M., *How Cosmic and Atmospheric Energies Influence Your Health*, Aurora Press, New York, 1981.

26. Hoyle, F., *The Intelligent Universe*, Michael Joseph, 1983.

27. Hoyle on Evolution. *Nature*, Vol. 294, November 1981.

28. Tillyard, E., *The Elizabethan World Picture*, Chatto & Windus, 1945.

29. Aquinas, St Thomas, *Summa Theologica*.

30. Gauquelin, M., *The Truth About Astrology*, Basil Blackwell, 1983.

31. ibid.

32. ibid.

33. Robbins, R., *An Encyclopedia of Witchcraft and Demonology*, Spring Books, London, 1964.

34. Gettings, F., *The Hidden Art*, Cassell, 1978.

35. For a clear objective discussion on the origins of Christianity see: Russell, B., *History of Western Philosophy*, George Allen & Unwin, 1946.

36. Hall, J., *A History of Ideas and Images in Italian Art*, John Murray, 1983.

37. Gettings, F., *The Hidden Art*, Cassell, 1978.

38. Hall, J., *A History of Ideas and Images in Italian Art*, John Murray, 1983.

39. Jung, C., His memorial address to Richard Wilhelm, contained in *The Secret of the Golden Flower*, Routledge & Kegan Paul, 1962.

40. Watson, L., *Supernature*, Hodder & Stoughton, 1979. And for a typically severe critique of Nelson's system, see Eysenck, H. & Nias, D., *Astrology, Science or Superstition?*, Maurice Temple Smith, 1982.

41. Seymour, P., *The Scientific Proof of Astrology*, Quantum/Foulsham 2004. And McGillion, F., 'The Pineal Gland and the Ancient Art of Iatromathematica', *Journal of Scientific Exploration*, Vol.16, no.1, 2002.

42. Dean, G. and others, *Recent Advances in Natal Astrology*, Analogic, Perth, 1977.

43. Watson, L., *Supernature*, Hodder & Stoughton, 1979.

44. Eysenck, H. & Nias, D., *Astrology, Science or Superstition?*, Maurice Temple Smith, 1982.

45. McGillion, F., *The Opening Eye*, Coventure Ltd., London, 1980. And for a thoroughly updated paper see McGillion, F., 'The Pineal Gland and the Ancient Art of Iatromathematica', *Journal of Scientific Exploration*, Vol.16, no.1, 2002. Or also in *Correlation*, Vol. 21, No.1, 2002/03.

46. ibid.

47. ibid.

48. ibid. And also Seymour, P., *The Scientific Proof of Astrology*, Quantum/ Foulsham, 2004.

49. ibid.

50. ibid.

51. Eysenck, H.J. & Nias, D.K.B., *Astrology, Science or Superstition?*, Maurice Temple Smith, 1982. And Watson, L., *Supernature*, Hodder & Stoughton, 1979.

52. ibid.

53. ibid.

54. McGillion, F., *The Opening Eye*, Coventure Ltd., London, 1980. And for a thoroughly updated paper see McGillion, F., 'The Pineal Gland and the Ancient Art of Iatromathematica', *Journal of Scientific Exploration*, Vol.16, no.1, 2002. Or also in Correlation, Vol. 21, No.1, 2002/03.

55. Gauquelin, M., *How Cosmic and Atmospheric Energies Influence Your Health*, Aurora Press, New York, 1981.

56. Eysenck, H.J. & Nias, D.K.B., *Astrology, Science or Superstition?*, Maurice Temple Smith, 1982. And Watson, L., *Supernature*, Hodder & Stoughton, 1979. And see also Gauquelin, M., *How Cosmic and Atmospheric Energies Influence Your Health*, Aurora Press, New York, 1981.

57. ibid. And also Seymour, P., *The Scientific Proof of Astrology*, Quantum/ Foulsham, 2004.

58. Kollerstrom, N., *Astrochemistry, a Study of Metal–Planet Affinities*, Emergence Press, 1984. And various papers in *The Astrological Journal*, XVIX no. 3, with Drummond, M. & Kollerstrom, N., XXIV no. 4.

59. ibid. And also Pelikan, W., *The Secrets of Metals*, trans. from the original German, Anthroposophical Press, 1973.

60. Capra, F., *The Tao of Physics*, Bantam, 1977. See also Barrow, J. & Tipler, F., *The Anthropic Cosmological Principle*, Oxford University Press, 1986.

61. Gauquelin, M., numerous original papers but summed up readily for the general reader, with references of course, in his book, *The Truth About Astrology*, Basil Blackwell, 1983.

62. ibid.

63. Research Group for the Critical Study of Astrology, United Kingdom – an independent research group based at the University of Southampton. www.astrology-research.net

64. Gauquelin, M., *How Cosmic and Atmospheric Energies Influence Your Health*, Aurora Press, New York, 1981.

65. Piccardi, G., *The Chemical Basis of Medical Climatology*, Thomas Books, Illinois, 1963. Or summed up easily in Gauquelin, M., *How Cosmic and Atmospheric Energies Influence Your Health*, Aurora Press, New York, 1981.

66. Jung, C., *Synchronicity: An Acausal Connecting Principle*, Routledge & Kegan Paul, 1955.

67. Barrow, J. & Tipler, F., *The Anthropic Cosmological Principle*, Oxford University Press, 1986.

68. The Sophia Project. Web: sophia-project.org.uk and The Kepler College of Astrological Arts and Sciences. USA. Web: www.kepler.edu

69. See any of the excellent volumes by the psychotherapist Liz Green, including *Relating, Saturn, The Astrology of Fate*, from Aquarian Press and others.

70. For those interested in this field, current research is now being co-ordinated by the Urania Trust and the Astrological Association. See list of useful addresses on page 000.

71. Palant, D., *The Astrological Journal,* XXV no. 2, and the Editorial of XXIX no. 4. Also see Arch Crawford's website http://crawfordperspectives.com

72. Watters, B., *Horary Astrology and the Judgement of Events,* Valhalla, 1973. And Barclay, O., *Horary Astrology Revisited,* Whitford Press, 1990. And for one of the best examples of all, see Barclay, O., *The Astrological Journal,* XXV no. 4, letters section, and the celebrated story of Max, the lost cat.

Chapter 9

1. ITC Program Code Revision. November 2003. There are always revisions of these codes going on. To check for the latest, visit the new organisation responsible (OFCOM) at www.ofcom.org.uk

2. Kollerstrom, N., *Astrochemistry, a Study of Metal–Planet Affinities,* Emergence Press, 1984.

3. www.astrology-and-science.com   Geofrey Dean's website contains routes to most of those studies that purport to have disproved the validity of astrology or to have discredited those experiments that have attempted to validate it. If you are an astrologer who believes astrology is a science, you should probably take a look.

Chapter 10

1. Lao Tzu, *Tao Te Ching,* trans. Ch'u Ta-Kao, George Allen & Unwin, 1959.

2. Obviously translations vary. Conventional biographers, however, are pretty consistent in their unwillingness to transmit Kepler's real views on the subject. Standard biographical works include: Caspar, M., *Kepler,* trans. Hellman, C.D., Abelard-Schumann, 1959. And Koestler, A., *Watershed: A Biography of Johannes Kepler,* Doubleday, 1960. See also Graubard, M., *Astrology's Decline and Its Bearing On the Decline and Death of Beliefs,* Osiris, 1958. And even the BBC's otherwise excellent Open University production on Kepler and his ideas.

3. Seymour, P., *The Scientific Proof of Astrology.* Quantum/Foulsham, 2004.

4. Lao Tzu, *Tao Te Ching,* trans. Gia-Fu Feng & English, J., Wilswood House, 1973.

Chapter 11

1. 'Objections to Astrology', a statement by 186 leading scientists, *Humanist* 35, no. 5, Sept/Oct 1975.

2. The journal *Aquarian Agent,* 1976.

3. Mayo, J., White, O. and Eysenck, H., *The Journal of Social Psychology,* 1978. Eysenck, H.J. & Nias, D.K.B., *Astrology, Science or Superstition?,* Maurice Temple Smith, 1982. And see also Jeff Mayo's defence of his later work and replications in *The Astrological Journal,* XXVIII nos. 4 and 5.

4. Carlson, S., 'A Double-Blind Test of Astrology', *Nature,* vol. 318, no. 6045, 1985.

5. *The Astrological Journal,* April 1986, describing a communication from T.W. Hamilton.

6. Gauquelin, M., *The Truth About Astrology*, Basil Blackwell, 1983. And abridged English translations of the original papers now available in Gauquelin's *Written in the Stars*, Aquarian, 1988.

7. Gauquelin, M., *The Truth About Astrology*, Basil Blackwell, 1983.

8. ibid.

9. Ertel. S., *Correlation, Astrological Association Journal of Research into Astrology*, Vol. 15, Issue 1, 1996. And more recently, Ertel & Irving, Journal of Scientific Exploration, Vol 14, No.3, 2000.

10. Dean, G. and others, *Recent Advances in Natal Astrology: A Critical Review 1900–1976*, Analogic, Perth, 1977.

11. Ertel. S, *Correlation, Astrological Association Journal of Research into Astrology*, Vol. 17, Issue 1, 1998.

12. Fuzeau-Braesch, S. *Correlation, Astrological Association Journal of Research into Astrology*, Vol. 19, Issue 2, 2000/01.

13. Kollerstrom, N., and Steffert, S., *BMC Psychiatry*, Vol. 3, No. 20, 2003.

Glossary of Terms

Ascendant This usually refers to the degree of the zodiac sign which is rising in the birth chart. In popular conversation, however, it can refer to the whole sign. It is of at least equal importance to the Sun sign when judging character.

Aspects Angular relationships within the chart that draw together the characters of the planets in certain ways. There are several aspects, each corresponding to an exact division of the circle. However, an allowance, or 'orb', of several degrees either side of exactitude is permitted, and it is the narrowness or otherwise of this orb which indicates the strength of the aspect itself.

Astrology The ancient art of determining character and forecasting events through judgement of celestial events.

Astronomy The scientific measurement of celestial phenomena. Speculation on the size, shape, age, etc., of the universe. Prior to the Renaissance, a term synonymous with astrology.

Celestial Equator The Earth's equator projected on to the sphere of the heavens. A great circle, therefore, at 90 degrees to the Earth's axis of rotation.

Chart An accurate map of the sky for the exact time and place of an event – usually a birth. The chart forms the basis of all serious astrological work.

Constellations Ancient star patterns still used by scientists as means of nomenclature. Although a constellation, say Pisces, can share the same name as the astrologer's sign 'Pisces', it has little to do with it except in historical terms.

Cusp Borderline. People 'born on the cusp' are those whose birthdays occur when the Sun is changing signs. A cusp in astrology also means the dividing line between houses as well as signs.

Ecliptic A great circle in the sky traced by the apparent motion of the Sun as the Earth orbits about it once every 365 days. The ecliptic is the centre-line of the zodiac, which ranges approximately eight degrees above and below it. The ecliptic is inclined to the Earth's equator at an angle of around 23 degrees, and it is this phenomenon that produces the cycle of the seasons.

Elements Each sign has its element, or mode of expression. Planets vary slightly in character according to the element in which each is found. In Western astrology we work with four elements: Fire, Earth, Air and Water.

Equinoctial Points Two places in the sky where the celestial equator cuts the ecliptic. The Sun positioned on these points indicates equal length of day and night anywhere on Earth, and the spring equinoctial point for the northern hemisphere always indicates the starting point of the zodiac, and consequently of the first sign, Aries.

Geocentric Earth-centred or in orbit about the Earth.

Heliocentric Sun-centred or in orbit about the Sun.

Horary The branch of astrology dealing with specific questions and the judgement of events. (Latin 'of the hour'.)

Houses Segments of the chart, twelve in number, and commencing at the Ascendant. Each house pertains to certain fields of activity, to certain people or places. For instance, the seventh house relates, among other things, to partners and rivals; the tenth house to career and parental influences. There is nothing in the world that is not covered by one of the twelve houses of astrology.

IC Abbreviation for the Latin Immum Coeli. The lowest point of the ecliptic in any chart, corresponding to due north at the location in question. Directly opposite the MC therefore.

MC Abbreviation for the Latin Medium Coeli, or the point where the ecliptic crosses the local meridian. In other words, due south on the zodiac.

Meridian Usually refers to the local meridian, or great circle that passes through the zenith (overhead) and the north and south points of the horizon.

Midpoint A point between two bodies in the chart. There are many of these, of course, but they are only relevant when a third body is contacted, either by conjunction or by aspect to that point. Midpoints can provide much additional detail in natal work and any worthwhile analysis should always at least consider them along with the more basic features of the chart.

Mundane Astrology Political astrology. Nations and people. Economics.

Polarity There are six positive and six negative signs in the zodiac, the terms being roughly synonymous with extraversion or introversion respectively, or the Yang and Yin of oriental philosophy. The characters of the planets can alter slightly according to the polarity of the sign in which each is found.

Planet Technically a planet is any large body in orbit about a star, including our own Sun, which is also a star, only very close. In astrology, however, both the Moon and the Sun are often termed 'planets'. The positions of such bodies are constantly changing in relation to the Earth, and it is this, along with the rotation of the Earth itself, that creates the many variables of astrology, moment to moment, chart to chart. The glyphs for the planets are as follows:

Sun	☉	Jupiter	♃
Moon	☽	Saturn	♄
Mercury	☿	Uranus	♅
Venus	♀	Neptune	♆
Mars	♂	Pluto	♇

Precession More fully: precession of the equinoxes. Due to a slight 'wobble' of the Earth's axis, rather like the wobble of a spinning top, the ecliptic circle moves around the celestial equator once every 22,000 years or so, taking the equinoctial points, and thus the zodiac itself, along with it. The zodiac is therefore seen to vary in relation to the background of fixed stars, or constellations as they are called. Around 2000 years ago, the signs and the constellations shared the same names and roughly the same places in the sky. Now, however, the zodiac signs have moved on, and the sign Aries has drifted into the section of the sky occupied by the stars of the ancient constellation of Pisces. This creates considerable confusion for the layperson. Astronomers and map makers, though, being perhaps more traditionally oriented than astrologers, have since the time of Ptolemy (second century AD) neglected to change the constellation boundaries to keep pace with precession.

Progressions Term used for the most popular method of forecasting. Positions in the progressed chart for any period are compared to natal positions to determine trends and developments.

Ruler Each sign, and also each house has what is called a 'ruler'. For example, the planet Mercury always rules the signs Gemini and Virgo. It can also rule one or more houses in the individual chart. This house rulership is determined by the location of the house cusp. If, say, your 7th house cusp falls in the sign Virgo (ruled by Mercury) then we know that the movements and relative strengths of Mercury will relate closely to all 7th house matters: in other words, partners or rivals.

Transit In astrology this usually means any situation where a planet's current position creates a cross aspect to a feature in a birth chart.

Zodiac A narrow band in the sky extending approximately eight degrees either side of the ecliptic, or annual path traced by the Sun. It is divided into twelve equal sections, or signs – echoing the hexagonal pattern found so often in nature: the snowflake, for example. The glyphs for the signs are written as follows:

Aries	♈	Taurus	♉	Gemini	♊
Cancer	♋	Leo	♌	Virgo	♍
Libra	♎	Scorpio	♏	Sagittarius	♐
Capricorn	♑	Aquarius	♒	Pisces	♓

Useful Addresses and URLs

If you wish to contact a good astrologer in your area, a school or a local group, but do not have a personal recommendation, then it may be worthwhile contacting one or more of the sources in the following list. However, note that many of these organisations do not have headquarters as such. They are often run by volunteers, and are usually non-profit making. So if you write requesting a reply or information, do please enclose a large stamped addressed envelope.

The Advisory Panel on Astrological Education, Web: www.apae.org.uk

American Federation of Astrologers, 6535 S. Rural Rd./ Tempe, AZ 85283-3746, USA. Web: www.astrologers.com

Association of Professional Astrologers International (APAI), Web: www.professionalastrologers.org

The Astrological Association of Great Britain, Unit 168, Lee Valley Technopark, Tottenham Hale, London N17 9LN. Web: www.astrologer.com/aanet/

The Astrological Lodge of London, Web: www.astrolodge.co.uk

The Centre for Psychological Astrology, Workshop and professional training program. BMC Box 1815, London WC1N 3XX. Web: www.cpalondon.com

Crawford Perspectives, Crawford Perspectives is a financial markets advisory service utilising technical analysis and planetary cycles research. It publishes a monthly newsletter, which has been edited by Arch Crawford since 1977. Web: http://crawfordperspectives.com

Faculty of Astrological Studies, Web: www.astrology.org.uk

Kepler College of Astrological Arts and Sciences. Degree course, USA. Web: www.kepler.edu

The Mayo School of Astrology, Alvana Gardens, Tregavethan, Truro, Cornwall TR4 9EN. Web: www.astrology-world.com/mayo

National Council for Geocosmic Research, USA. Web: www.geocosmic.org

Research Group for the Critical Study of Astrology, Web: www.astrology-research.net

The Sophia Project, independent organisation to advance the study of astrology and cultural astronomy in British institutions of higher education. Web: www.sophia-project.org.uk

The Traditional Horary Course. For those who wish to learn the art of horary astrology. Continues the outstanding work of the late Olivia Barclay. E-mail: sueward@easynet.co.uk

The Urania Trust, E-mail: uraniatrust@f2s.com

Finally, if you have enjoyed this book, you may also like to visit the author's website: www.astralogos.wanadoo.co.uk

Suggested Reading List

CAPRA, F., *The Tao of Physics*, Flamingo, 1992. An eminent scientist discussing the similarities between particle physics and mysticism.

CARTER, C., *The Principles of Astrology*, Theosophical Publishing House Ltd., 1925. An old book, but still one of the best introductions to the subject available, if you can get it.

GAUQUELIN, M., *How Cosmic and Atmospheric Energies Influence Your Health*, Aurora Press, New York, 1981. Meteorology and astronomy combine here to make fascinating reading.

GAUQUELIN, M., *The Truth About Astrology*, Basil Blackwell, 1983. A good, all-round summary for the general reader of the work of this remarkable man.

GETTINGS, F., *The Hidden Art*, Cassell, 1978. The first few chapters dealing with the esoteric dimension of Christian art are superb.

HALL, M.P., *The Secret Teachings of All Ages*, The Philosophical Research Society, USA, 1977. Also published more recently through Jeremy P. Tarcher Reader's Edition, USA, 2003. A wonderfully illustrated and comprehensive guide to the mystical dimension of world religions and occult teachings.

HOYLE, F., *The Intelligent Universe*, Michael Joseph, London, 1983. The late Sir Fred Hoyle, one of the world's leading astrophysicists, explains his research into genetics and the dramatic conclusions that seriously question the accepted view of life on Earth.

LANDSCHEIDT, *Sun-Earth-Man*, The Urania Trust, 1989. A wonderfully holistic tour of astrology as it pertains to culture, climate, economics and much, much more. Original and thought-provoking.

LAO TZU, *Tao Te Ching*, trans. Ch'u Ta-Kao, George Allen & Unwin, 1959. The great Chinese classic of wisdom and Taoist philosophy. There are many translations but this seems as good, if not better, than most.

MAYO, J., *The Astrologer's Astronomical Handbook,* Fowler, 1979. A book of this kind provides a sound technical background for astrologers.

McGILLION, F., *The Opening Eye,* Coventure, London, 1993. Discussion of the pineal gland and its sensitivity to cosmic phenomena.

PARRY, R., *Teach Yourself Chi Kung,* Hodder, 2001. Sometimes we need to take care of our body in order to be able to function well in the brain!

PARRY, R., *Baby Names and Star Signs,* Hamlyn/Pyramid, 2004. Inspired by the ancient system of correspondences and symbolism, this is an entertaining look at the meaning of names from the perspective of astrology.

PARRY, R., *Tai Chi for Health and Vitality,* Hamlyn, 2005. About the art of relaxation.

SEYMOUR, P., *The Scientific Proof of Astrology,* Quantum, 2004. Written by a former principle lecturer in astronomy and astrophysics. Intelligent speculation and some persuasive theories about a possible working hypothesis for astrology.

And for the more specialist reader:

CAMPION, N. The Book of World Horoscopes, Wessex Astrologer Ltd, 2004. An excellent source book for mundane astrologers and those interested in world history and political affairs.

ERTEL, S. & IRVING, K., *The Tenacious Mars Effect,* The Urania Trust, 1996. Continuing the pioneering work of Gauquelin by providing evidence against the findings of those who have sought to discredit his work. Debunking the debunkers – who have, it has to be said, been debunked themselves by others who have, themselves been debunked ... and so on. The debate rages on. Intelligent and worthy reading for those engaged in research into astrology or those seeking scientific respectability for astrology.

EYSENCK, H. & NIAS, D., *Astrology, Science or Superstition?*, The Urania Trust, 1982. Extremely thorough and well researched book by two eminent statisticians. Eysenck tends to give the benefit of the doubt to the sceptics rather than to the astrologer, but otherwise this book brings welcome clarity to what is often a notoriously woolly subject.

ROBERTS, P. & GREENGRASS, H., *The Astrology of Time Twins*, The Pentland Press, 1994 – also available through the Urania Trust (see Useful Addresses section). A large study of the phenomenon of time twins. Although it has its critics – namely those who always criticise studies suggesting any kind of validity to astrology – it is a impressive body of work. Of great value for anybody considering taking up astrological research.

Index